TEACHING TO MAKE SUCCESS UNAVOIDABLE IN THE ELEMENTARY SCHOOL

An Educational Plan to Correct the Problems of
Social Promotion in the Elementary School

By Frank H. Meyers, Ph.D.

ISBN 13: 978-1-935986-98-0

LIBERTY
UNIVERSITY
PRESS

Published by Liberty University Press. Printed in the U.S.A.
Liberty University Press
1971 University Blvd.
Lynchburg, VA 24515

www.Liberty.edu/LibertyUniversityPress
First trade paperback edition, July 2014
All scripture quotations, unless otherwise indicated, are taken from the Liberty Annotated Study Bible, King James Version
Copyright 1988 by Liberty University
and NIV as identified. — *Holy Bible, New International Version*®. Copyright © 1973, 1978, 1984
by International Bible Society. Used by permission of Zondervan Publishing House. All rights reserved.

DEDICATION

This book is dedicated to all of the students who were socially promoted to the next grade in elementary schools and were not educated on their instructional levels in language arts and basic mathematics. They went up to middle and high schools without mastering these two subjects which handicapped them in all their future learning. Some had to take one or two additional years to complete high school or dropped out of school along the way which led to bad behavior, drugs, crime and even incarcerations. The AUG Plan was conceived to correct the problems caused by social promotion which had no successful plan to teach students on their instructional levels in language arts and basic mathematics after they were socially promoted.

In addition, this book is dedicated to all the teachers who were given impossible teaching tasks of students who were not on grade level and had not mastered language arts and/or basic mathematics. The AUG Plan was conceived to provide an educational plan that would make success unavoidable for all students.

I also dedicate the book to my family. My wife Shirley; son and his wife, Frank T. and Jennifer M. Meyers; daughter and her husband, Sheri M. and Yiannakis C. Tittiris; grandsons and their wives, Daniel Y. and Michelle S. Tittiris, Timothy Y. and Cynthia E. Tittiris and grandson, Joshua A. Tittiris and granddaughter, Stephanie J. Tittiris.

ACKNOWLEDGEMENTS

My thanks goes to William R. Dean who prepared me well in writing papers on the graduate level; David Culler for support relating to the computer; Rosemary Culler for assistance in typing part of the manuscript; and proofreaders Shirley B. Meyers, Sheri M. Tittiris; Sarah A. Funderburke, and her staff.

I am indebted to many family members, friends, educators and parents through the years who when they heard of the AUG Plan for teaching students in the elementary schools in a way which makes success unavoidable in language arts and basic mathematics, encouraged me to put the plan into book form. Without their support the project would not have been completed.

THE PURPOSE OF THIS BOOK

The plan was conceived in 1978 and put into effect in an elementary school for four years. For years the plan has been verbally shared with educators and school board members but without seeing the plan implemented. This book is long overdue. The purpose was to provide an educational plan that would prepare students for success in all future learning. It will help solve the problems caused by social promotion and not result in grade failure in the elementary, middle and high schools and correct the practice of students being sent up to higher grades unprepared to handle the subject matter.

TABLE OF CONTENTS

Section Five Conclusions

PREFACE

Managing the Mess

In the great scheme of life, there is not much that could be more important than the educational foundation that we give to our children. Let's face it, education is the one thing that will determine the success and normally, the salary that one earns once they get out into the real world to get a job and start a family.

Education should be the one thing that teaches children facts, and teaches children to evaluate the facts, draw conclusions about the facts, and apply the facts to the situations that they find themselves in life. With a good education comes more choices and opportunities in life.

In America, our educational system is so dysfunctional. We teach to a multiple choice bubble test, and we wonder why the kids who graduate do not know how to work together and problem solve. We pit teacher against teacher in the name of teacher bonuses for student achievement, which on the surface sounds great. But when you break it all down without looking at the needs of each child in the classroom and the issues that the child brings into the classroom each day, some achievements just cannot be seen on the typical standardized test that measures what a child did on one test on one particular day.

Children who have grown up in impoverished neighborhoods have fewer chances of getting a good education. Typically, they score lower on tests, and have fewer opportunities in going to college. Without addressing the issues of poverty, family life, and educational needs of the parents, these children have little chance in the real world in pulling themselves out of the poverty cycle—and the rest of us will complain about "the welfare class" that ends up as the result of our lack of being successful in educating our youth.

To draw this point out, consider the following scenario. Johnny is in 5th grade. His mom is a single parent of two kids. Johnny has no father figure in his life. Johnny goes to school tired, because he has worked hard helping his younger brother at home while mom works to support the family. Johnny struggles with reading, because his mom does not have extra money to buy books for the kids and little time to take them to the library due to the time demands in her life. Due to his lack of reading, Johnny struggles with reading. Due to the lack of money, Johnny does not go to the movies, theater, and vacations; so his understanding of vocabulary is limited due to his lack of personal experience with the words that he is learning in his vocabulary. Johnny also has a learning disability called dyslexia, which went undiagnosed, due to the lack of special education testing in the public school system.

In a typical school, most school systems will not look favorably on labeling a student with a learning disability until third grade, which puts the child even further behind in their reading abilities due to the time lost due to the teacher's lack of support in dealing with the child's specific learning disability. Because of this lack, Johnny is taught to read in the traditional way, instead of using the special techniques utilized in teaching dyslexia. This struggle then translates to all other courses, since reading is the foundation for education.

Now tell me, in this situation, is it the child's 4th or 5th grade teacher's fault that Johnny is having difficulty passing the state mandated testing? In education, we love to play the blame game. Parents and politicians blame the teachers and the tenure system. Teachers blame the parents and the lack of funding. Not any one of these groups want to acknowledge that the real failure of the public school system is a general failure of our overall society in general. So, to solve the problem, politicians have come up with idiotic measures like "No Child Left Behind" and "Race to the Top." Really, in NCLB, the law actually states that all students will be performing at grade level in Math and reading by 2014. This includes non-English speaking students and special education students with severe disabilities such as autism, developmentally delayed students, and students with learning disabilities. Is this really right or fair?

To solve the problems in our educational system, we are going to have to tackle many social, economical, and personal issues that these students and their families are dealing with. There are high school students who are homeless and receive NO ASSISTANCE, and we wonder why school is such a low priority or why these kids drop out.

So, in closing, before we play the blame game, let's look at the actual nature of the problem. Let's look at how these issues affect the child, and their educational experience. Most teachers that I know do the job because of their love of kids and learning, not for long summer breaks and the huge paycheck they get twice a month. They do it to make a difference. We are proud when we succeed against the odds, and disappointed and ashamed when we don't. I really wish the politicians would come up with a plan to reform education that would build teamwork among the teachers, enabling support and respect among the teachers and parents, rather than one which pits the two against one another. I wish they would encourage parental support in helping educate the parents in what is expected of them at home with homework help, helping connect with financial assistance and the like, rather than building tension between parents and teachers. Who knows, maybe if we all learned to support one another, and address the emotional, physical, social, and educational needs of the family as a whole, we just might reach some of those lofty goals set by the politicians. -Anonymous

INTRODUCTION

Many people are very familiar with the writings of Laura Ingalls Wilder and the ungraded one room school house which was in use in the early days of rural American and Canadian schools. Along with Laura Wilder, the following all had their early education in one-room school-houses: Herbert Hoover, Joyce Carol Oates and Alan B. Shepherd, Jr.[1] The invention of motorized school buses in the 1920's, made possible the transportation of students and the beginning of the multiple classrooms where classes could be held separately.

As cities grew in student population the graded schools became popular. In 1948, many rural areas had ungraded schools due to the sparse population of students. In Canada, the rural schools had enrollments of 21–24 students and one teacher for grades 1–8. Here is an example of how one teacher planned his day in teaching 22 students in grades 1–8.

Rural Ungraded Schools In Canada
by Harry G. Peters, Retired Elementary School Teacher

In 1948, my teaching career began in an ungraded rural school in Southwestern Ontario. In one classroom, it was my responsibility to present curricula, as mandated to students enrolled in each grade from 1 to 8 inclusive.

Over six decades later, I have been asked to evaluate the effectiveness of teaching methods in the ungraded setting. In review, I did indeed, find considerable differences in the following 35 years while I taught in graded schools.

I clearly recall beginning each day in the ungraded school by focusing my instruction for at least 90 minutes on students in Grades 1 and 2 by drilling previously taught concepts and mastering new material in Reading and Mathematics.

After school closing each day, I prepared a schedule on the chalkboard for the following day, showing the "time and topic" responsibilities of students in Grades 3–8 during times when they would not be receiving grade-specific instruction in small groups. I delivered this instruction as teacher, at the front of the classroom from a small platform on which my desk stood. Although the students in other grade levels were working on their assignments, this teaching model provided them exposure and introduction to concepts at a higher learning level simply by osmosis. Conversely, students who had advanced to higher grades benefited from the inexorable exposure to remedial teaching by their presence in the ungraded environment.

Accordingly, following opening exercises, I could give attention to students of Grade 1 and 2 while students of higher grades proceeded independently with seat work related assignments as outlined on the schedule.

During later parts of a school day, students of Grades 3–8 who showed efficiency and dependability in completion and mastery in their studies, were often asked to help primary students read and to monitor completion of their seat work.

As I recall the 35 years of teaching in graded schools, which followed my initial year in the "rural school," the difference in the level of independence of students in the ungraded schools remains distinct. It was necessary, in the graded schools, to develop strategies to counteract the tendency of students to be less attentive to lessons and to rely on personal explanations of problems by the teacher or another student.

Additionally, fellow teachers agreed that former students from ungraded schools were well represented among leadership positions in areas of education, commerce, finance and other professions.

Not to be overlooked in the evaluation is the contribution obviously necessary of teachers whose skills and flexibility put into action the presentation of curricula in such a manner that student independence was the inevitable result.

I talked with Mr. Peters recently and found out that many educators observed that students from the rural ungraded school setting made good transitions when they reached high school in graded schools. Many of these students went on to become very successful leaders in their future endeavors. In the rural setting they learned to help other students to become successful in their studies. Those who knew the material helped those who were having trouble learning. The caring attitude they displayed was carried over to the high school days and throughout life.

If students are taught to master units in reading, many will become independent readers by the end of third grade. Others will reach that goal by the end of fifth grade, if they are taught in a way that makes success in reading an unavoidable goal by the end of fifth grade. The purpose of this book is to show how easy it is to accomplish this goal by making sure no gaps are formed in a child's education in language arts and basic mathematics.

PROLOGUE

American education was based on belief in God. The early reading books used to educate America's children were the *McGuffey's Readers*[2]. They were among the first textbooks designed to become progressively more challenging with each volume. They were printed in 1849, and were used in the one room schoolhouses. When the nation became more pluralistic in the late 1860s, they were slowly taken out of the schools. This happened after Charles Darwin published *Origin of Species* in 1859.

Students have not changed much since the 1800s. Every student is unique – one of a kind. This makes each one valuable and special. They had no input into their birth. And yet many people treat these valuable individuals with little or no consideration or respect.

Mankind is part of God's creation and is commanded to love God with all their heart, soul and mind, (Deut. 6:5); to love one another as Christ loved us, (John 15:12); to love our neighbor as ourself, (Lev. 19:18); to love our enemies, bless them that curse you, do good to them that hate you and to pray for them that despitefully use you and persecute you, (Matt. 5:44). God said to Moses, "Who made man's mouth? Or who makes him dumb or deaf or seeing or blind? Is it not I, the Lord," (Ex. 4:11). Who are we to treat others badly when God has given us His Golden Rule, "Therefore, all things whatsoever you would that men should do to you, do you even so to them: for this is the law and the prophets," (Matt. 7:12).

The educational plan presented on these pages is based on mutual respect and regard for all students regardless of their abilities or limitations. Educators must do everything within their power to give a just and meaningful education to all with no discrimination or prejudice.

The classrooms and/or homerooms are no places for bigotry, prejudice or discrimination by students or teachers. Teachers are there to educate students, and students are there to be taught on their instructional levels. By giving them a solid foundation in language arts and basic mathematics, they are prepared to be successful in all further education, which will follow them throughout life.

Who are we to blame God, parents, students or others for the way students come to us?   We should accept, educate and assist students in becoming all they can be in order to make this world a better place for all people.

SECTION ONE
SEARCH OF THE LITERATURE
(CHAPTERS 1– 4)

CHAPTER I

THE PROBLEMS OF SCHOOL FAILURE RESULTING IN LOW STUDENT PERFORMANCE

If one can identify where the problems of low student performance began, then one can know where to correct these problems that are making the public schools and other schools ineffective with so many of their students.

In the American school system, there are two foundational subjects that all students must master in order to be adequately prepared for all future learning. The subjects are:

• language arts, which includes English, reading, writing, and spelling.

• basic mathematics, which includes counting, addition, subtraction, multiplication, division, fractions and measurements.

Without mastery in any one of these subjects, students will have difficulty handling middle and high school work. One reason schools are in dire circumstances is because the elementary schools have failed to properly instruct students for mastery in each of these subjects. Many students are sent up to middle schools without mastery in these two subjects. If the problem is not solved in the middle schools, these students are sent up to high schools unprepared.

For the most part, the exit exam is the instrument that indicates whether or not students have mastered language arts and basic mathematics. Students who are not proficient in these two subjects will have problems in passing the exit exam.

Until the problems are corrected, students will continue to bring down national test scores, not only in the eighth and twelfth grades but also every year state tests are given. The exit exams reveal students who are very weak in language arts and/or basic mathematics.[3, 4] The problems starts in the elementary school.

Problems In Elementary Education

Test scores in language arts and basic mathematics in schools are below 1992 test scores.[5] This results in many problems, not only for the elementary schools, but also for the middle and high schools as seen by the state, national test scores and the published sources included in this book.

• Could it be that teachers' expectations are a cause for students' low test scores? Research has shown that teacher expectations have a major influence on how well students preform on these tests. If teachers think students are able to understand concepts that are being taught, and students are not understanding the concepts, the teachers will work harder to help them understand. On the other hand, if teachers think the students are unable to understand the material and move on to the next concepts, students will perform poorly. Teacher expectation has an important role to play in student's successful learning.[6]

• Could it be that social promotion has caused learning gaps to result because students were not mastering language arts or basic mathematics before being promoted? Is this another reason why one sees lower test scores? Whatever was not taught in the sending grades may never be covered in the receiving grades. These gaps continue to grow each passing year. The state and national testing is always done on-grade-level. Some students are not on-grade-level. Their test scores will always be lower for those grades.

• Could it be that schools do not have an adequate educational plan to teach socially promoted students on their instructional levels in language arts and basic mathematics? For many years schools have used social promotion in order to keep students with age-mates and have omitted academic achievement.[7] This resulted in the learning gaps which placed students at a disadvantage in future education because the gaps were never filled. There has not been a cost efficient way to prevent these learning gaps to continue without having to hire additional teachers.

• Could it be that mastering language arts and basic mathematics has not been taken seriously by the schools? But there may be no state laws making this a requirement for elementary schools. However, there are many things that schools are mandated to do by state law.[8] Some of these are: emergency drill is conducted during the first month of school (R43-166), fire drill at least once a month (59-63-910), immunization records are current for each student (44-29-180), 180 days in attendance, hurricane and tornado drills, and special monthly emphases, just to name a few requirements relating to schools. Why have elementary schools failed in teaching all students to master language arts and basic mathematics before sending them on to the middle schools?

• Could more money correct the problems that come up? Over and over again taxpayers are asked to give schools more money to correct the problem of low test scores. It may involve hiring more teachers to lower the teacher-students ratios. Sometimes it involves hiring consultants to find and recommend plans to correct the situations. Or it might involve paying for a program that will help to improve what is being taught and how it is being taught to increase test score results. All this can cost huge sums of money that taxpayers have to come up with through higher school taxes.

• Could it be that there is no evidence of the effectiveness of funds state or federal grants provide to correct the problems? The money is spent, but the problems are not solved; because the causes of the problems have not been removed.

Today the problems still exist. Students are not taught language arts and/or basic mathematics. Some students are promoted unprepared for the receiving grades. The receiving teacher is given an impossible task which cannot be solved because no plan has been put in place to teach students at their instructional levels in language arts and basic mathematics. Teachers receive students below, on and above grade level. It is an impossible task to teach language arts and basic mathematics to all these students. Each student would get 1/3 or less instructional time in each of these subjects.

There are schools that have not been able to meet their yearly goals. There are schools that will lose huge sums of money over changing student's test scores.[9]

• Could the problem be intellectual discrimination? Many schools in the past have had a three tier approach to classroom placement. Each grade had a class for above-average, average and below-average students. The above-average students may have received the academic attention. The below-average students may have received the least academic attention and may have come from homes where English was not the main language, the family was low socio-economic, or where there was little educational encouragement.

School Closings

One can see what is happening in schools throughout the United States. The number of schools that are being closed each year because of poor student performance is increasing every year. There has not been any successful method to correct the problems and stop the closing of neighborhood schools. What is happening? "Consortium on Chicago School Research (CCSR) found 82% of students from 18 elementary schools closed in Chicago moved from one underperforming school to another underperforming school including schools already on probation."[10]

If these students were moved to high performing schools, the test results of those schools would be lowered because the incoming students are very weak in these two subjects and little effort has been made to get them educated in the areas of their weaknesses. A school district is not doing its job when there are schools within the district that are not educating students to master language arts and basic mathematics. When students have learned the basics, they are ready for middle and high schools. Sending students into the middle and high schools without adequate preparation is the main reason for low test scores caused by the failure of the elementary schools to educate students in language arts and basic mathematics.

Some School Closings

Many states have schools that have been closed. Following are some of the states that have permanently closed schools. The closings can be the result of lack of students, students who are not adequately prepared for the receiving grades, buildings that are not fit for students and/or districts that want to have charter schools replace traditional, community schools.

Massachusetts: Massachusetts is one of the leading states in education. However, there was one school district where two high schools in Malden were facing closure in 2011. "Lawrence Public School district had 13,000 students, 90% were Hispanic, living in poverty and having trouble speaking and reading English. They were in the 1% range in reading and math."[11]

Chicago: "The Chicago Teachers' Union reported African Americans made up nearly 40% of all teachers in the 1990s. By 2012, that proportion was reduced to under 20%."[12] "Chicago is one of a number of cities that does not have recall rights for laid off employees."[13] "Sixty five percent of teachers laid off were African American women."[14]

After intervention those hired were younger and inexperienced. What that means is new teachers can be hired at a lower rate than experienced teachers who make much more financially because of their education levels. For example, beginning teachers with a B.A. make about $49.2K a year and teachers with a M.A. make about $86.2K a year.[15]

Chicago closed 49 elementary schools and one high school in June, 2013. Of the nearly 850 laid-off employees, 550 were teachers.[16] Students were reassigned and have to travel to many schools outside their neighborhoods. Over 90% of students from closed Chicago schools did not go to 'academically strong' new schools.[17] Marisa de la Torre, a director at the CCRS, has conducted research showing that "significan't academic improvement only occurred when displaced students transferred to the best schools."[18]

New Orleans, LA: After Katrina flooded the city of New Orleans, the schools were closed due to the damage suffered in the storm. Then came Rita. Before the storms, "sixty-two per cent of public schools were considered failing."[19] "Today students and educators have unprecedented leeway to mold educational experiences. Students can apply to and, if accepted, choose to attend any of the 46 charter schools or 23 'traditional' schools."[20] In the past over 60% of the schools were failing. Now only about 30% are failing schools in New Orleans. Even in traditional schools, principals have unusual autonomy over the hiring and firing of teachers, since the city's teachers' union lost its collective bargaining rights.[21]

The major cause for the closings of the majority of schools is students are not being taught language arts and/or basic mathematics on their instructional levels.

Charter Schools

Many school districts are encouraging charter schools in their districts. This move is something far removed from the concept of neighborhood schools and public education. "Public education means a tuition-free, publicly funded system that must provide an education to each child in a neighborhood school within a publicly governed school system. The academic standards, the teachers and administrators, the values and methods of operation employed in these schools are all subject to oversight and direction by public policy-making bodies. The rights of students and parents are legally defined and are enforceable by the courts."[22] This is not true of the charter schools.

"The charter schools are not under the authority of the school districts and operate much like a private business, free from many state laws and district regulations and perform about the same or worse compared to their traditional public school; (46% same, 37% worse and 17% better.)"[23] "They are supported by public funds from the school districts at a lower rate than the public schools. Some are run by boards with active parent involvement, while others are managed by corporations. Students attend by choice. Instead of supporting public schools, the corporate privatizers simply want to close them and open them as charter schools or walk away from schools, abandoning the communities as well."[24]

As one can see, many public schools are failing to properly educate students in elementary schools. This results in many students not being able to read on grade level and not being able to pass middle and high school math courses. An example is the high school valedictorian who could not pass the exit exam because she did not know language arts. When students have mastered language arts in the elementary schools, they can properly handle middle and high school courses. This weakness followed the student until she took the exit exam and could not pass the graduation test.[25]

Exit Exams

The best revealer that is letting people know how well the schools are doing in educating students is the exit exam.[26] The numbers of students that do not pass the exit exams is alarming. These tests indicate how well students have learned skills in reading, math and English. The foundations for these subjects must be mastered in the elementary schools or students are going to have major problems in handling middle and high school work. Because the problem began in the elementary schools, it must be corrected in the elementary schools. The middle and high schools will have to work with students who have not mastered language arts and basic mathematics in order for the test scores to go up. Instead of teachers teaching students how to pass state tests, they must make sure they have mastered language arts and basic mathematics in the elementary schools.

Middle and High Schools.

Middle and High Schools have to identify students who have not mastered language arts and basic mathematics in the elementary school. Until the AUG Plan is followed in the elementary school, middle and high schools are going to continue to receive students who have not mastered the basics of these two subjects. The exit exam will quickly identify these students.

Lastly, could there be some other causes that have not been addressed at this time? Every effort must be made to insure that all students will receive an educational foundation which will allow them to do well throughout all their school years.

CHAPTER 2

THE DATA REPORTS ON SCHOOLS, STUDENTS, AND SUBJECT LEARNING

A wealth of material is available on students' learning of different subjects (language arts, mathematics, science, state and national testing, ACT and SAT scores.)   The middle school teachers lament that by the time many students get to them, they are not ready for grade level work.   There is no educational plan in the elementary schools to adequately correct the situation. Many adjustments have been made but the problem still exists.

Many teachers are overwhelmed by the numbers of students not meeting basic education requirements. It all begins in the elementary school. Receiving teachers are just not able to give individual attention to each student to catch them up. Whenever teachers fail to have their students meet basic education standards for their grades, they are doing a great disservice to all who do not meet the standards and are promoted to the next grade. Teachers must be held accountable for preparing students for the next grade.

Reading

Reading exposure begins in preschool.[27] By kindergarten students should have a beginning knowledge of basic reading—recognize alphabet, able to make correct sounds, read grade level texts, create rhyming words, use phonetic skills, have awareness of print concepts, use language structure to read new words and display comprehension of what is being read. Being able to read is one of the most important skills in getting an education. It is the key for all future learning.

A study in 821 1st grade classrooms in 700 schools from 32 states found only 23% were judged high quality, 28% mediocre, and 17% low overall quality. It was a 17 year long research study of Early Child Care and Youth Development. (April 4, 2007).[28]

Language Arts

What language should be used in schools in America? English. There is research that suggests it is not the right thing to do.[29] But is that realistic? In the schools of France, it is French; in Germany, it is German; in Spain, it is Spanish; in Russia, it is Russian. In the schools of America it should also be English.

For any one living in America, it is extremely important that one know English. In the schools of America, English must be the main language. It should be taught in a way for students to be able to go home and teach their families how to use the English language.

There is no problem in teaching other languages, but to be able to become independent in America, one must know the language. The schools are the best place to have homes exposed to the language through the students.

Language involves not only speaking but also writing. Writing skills have decreased over the last ten years. Demand for good writers requires more time and attention devoted to writing instruction and assessments.[30] It is missing in many schools today.

Basic Mathematics

The second most important elementary school subject is basic mathematics. In talking with middle and high school math teachers, one hears that students are not prepared for their courses. Unless all students master basic mathematics they cannot handle middle and high school math.

It is common to hear high school teachers say some students do not know how to count. They must master basic mathematics before they can handle middle and high school math. Many do not know their multiplication tables in order to do Algebra. This also applies to middle school math. Teachers say the reasons students drop out of middle and high schools math is because they have not mastered the basics. Students must master basic mathematics in the elementary school before they can handle middle and high school maths. Mastering basic mathematics is a prerequisite to middle and high school maths.

Science

Science should not be straight identification, memorization of obscure names, technical, just reading, or diluted content.[31, 32] It should be study of one's physical and biological environment, development of problem solving, the acquisition of attitudes which are termed scientific such as accuracy, curiosity, and intellectual honesty. It should not be studying what one already knows but experiments to find new information. As one moves up in grades, small groups within the classes should work on hands-on experiments to gain new knowledge, so says Robert J. Wallace.[33]

State tests and national tests

State tests are expensive and have findings that are only valid within each state. It is impossible to compare one states' schools with another. The biggest problem is that they take valuable instructional time from necessary subjects that should be taught. The public does not need state tests to know that schools are failing to properly teach students. It is an unnecessary burden to have them trained to teach state testing when they are already qualified to teach school curriculum. The colleges have not trained them to do that. They prepared them to teach subject matter.

Standardized tests are expensive and have failed to offer news one needs about students and specific curricular objectives. So far they have not helped to improve our schools. They only assess a narrow range of the curriculum, focus neither on aptitude nor specific curricular objects and yield results that apply only to state or nation and not to individual students or schools.

What is needed is a national test of subject content that can yield information in which to compare one state with others in how well students do on each subject. That would yield a valid indicator in comparing one state with other states. It would also provide sound data on achievement not just aptitude, and cause schools to focus on important performance-based outcomes and yield results for every level of the educational system about all students.[34]

The ACT and SAT national tests are good in looking at individual students and their performances. This also applies to comparing schools on how well their students do on these tests.

CHAPTER 3

THE QUESTION OF TEACHER EVALUATIONS

With all the problems in the educational system today, there are those who want to give teachers a failing grade if students do not perform up to the standards. It is time to step back and see wherein lies the major problems. Years ago a tenured professor at a leading university made the following statement in case it was decided to grade teachers on the basis of performance. He said that was fine with him as long as he got to pick his students.

Think of leaders that are given a task and are allowed to pick their co-workers. It is done all the time. Why not do that with teachers? This would be fair, would it not, for teachers to get to choose their students if they are going to be graded on performance?

The Problem, Schools Have No Educational Plan To Correct It

Let's look at teachers and the tasks they have to perform on the students given to them each year. They have no input in the choice of students they get. Is it fair to hold them responsible and not give them an educational plan that will assure them a successful year?

This is what is happening year after year. Students are placed in rooms with no thought given to their instructional levels. And the results are always the same. Receiving teachers are getting many students who are not prepared for their educational needs to be met. When are school boards, administrators and people that make the placement decisions and curriculum schedules going to change what they are doing to give teachers an environment which is a win, win for all – students, teachers, administrators, district personnel and parents? It is time for such a plan to be implemented in every school.

Grading teachers

Is it not time to grade parents, district boards, school administrators and those who set up the school's schedules as well as teachers? We already grade the students. Before we grade teachers, put yourself in their shoes. Would you want to be graded as a fully certified professional when you cannot do what you were trained to do because of regulations that keep you from doing that?

Were teachers trained to teach students how to take the mandated state tests? Nowhere in the state regulations does one see such a mandate. Why is so much time wasted that could help students progress in their education?

Do not fire teachers

A principal had a teacher who was weak in a few areas and recommended that the teacher be transferred out of the school. The replacement that came in was more of a problem than the one transferred out. The principal said that it would have been better to keep the former teacher and give in-service training in the areas of weakness. Then, if there were no improvement, to recommend the teacher be revaluated to see where one could be placed in the system.

One major problem in working with tenured teachers is they cannot be fired. It would be better to provide in-service in the areas of their weaknesses and/or place them according to their abilities. These teachers have met the basic requirements for employment.

Teacher evaluations

One state is working on a new evaluation system for teachers and administrators that could result in failing grades. At the end of the year, it could be teachers or principals getting an A or an F.[35]

When the State School Administrators Association does a survey, typically 400 to 500 educators respond. This time 18,000 educators responded to the issue of teacher evaluations, and they were not happy.[36] One point that raised the most concern was basing a decision on "value added." There is an over reliance on a test score given at one point and not a lot of other growth factors. It is down to where did students start and where did they finish.

Under the present plans, many teachers are given classes with huge differences in where students are in language arts and basic mathematics. There is no human way any one teacher can handle the teaching environment with success. The ranges of differences are too great. The ones who suffer the most are those below grade-level students.

Value Added Modeling

Value Added Modeling (VAM) is being considered to use in evaluating teachers and principals. The concept has been debunked by the president of Math for America, Dr. John Ewing who wrote, "Those promoting it are ill-equipped to judge either its effectiveness or its limitations." Further he states, "mathematics that ought to be used to illuminate ends up to intimate."[37] Years ago tests indicated to parents how well students were doing in school. Today tests have more consequences.

Donald T. Campbell said, "The more any quantitative social indicator is used for social decision-making, the more subject it will be to corruption pressures and the more it will be to distort and corrupt the social processes it tends to measure." (Campbell, 1976).[38] High-stakes tests are likely to induce some people to cheat.[39] The cause of school problems may not be the teachers but the way students are assigned to classes.

Before teachers are evaluated, let's correct the major problems

If administrators are going to evaluate teachers, they must provide an educational plan that will create environments where teachers can be successful all the time. That means below-grade-level students are going to have all their needs met. Also all above-grade-level students are going to have their needs met. Right now the only ones that are having their needs met are the average students. But they are paying a tremendous price because they only receive one third of the time. One third of the instructional time is given to below-grade-level students and one third of the time is given to above-grade-level students. But is that an ideal situation for all students. In the homerooms, all students have to settle for less and not more instructional time.

The learning environment should be fixed before one talks about teacher evaluations. One may be surprised to see that the new plan may solve the major problems in education today. With a new plan, it may greatly reduce one's concerns about evaluating the teachers. Correct the impossible tasks classroom teachers have and notice the increased learning that takes place in the school. A school district could save up to $3 million if the teaching environment were corrected.[40]

Parent Trigger Laws

In recent years, parents have had to put up with failing schools. Laws have been passed in a number of states to give parents more control about schools that fail to demonstrate academic achievement among students according to predetermined benchmarks such as test scores. A majority of parents can determine if principals and teachers should be dismissed and a new staff be brought in. The laws are called Parent Trigger Laws.[41]

All of this underscores the urgency for schools to make the necessary needed changes to improve the academic achievement of all students. It is all about properly teaching students in an environment that makes success unavoidable for all students. It can be done. The "how" answer is in this book.

CHAPTER 4

THE PROBLEMS WITH TEST SCORES AND THE CONFUSION THEY CREATE

Millions of tax dollars are being spent to evaluate the effectiveness of educational objectives, standards, teaching, assessments, and accountability in elementary, middle, and high schools in America by state and federal governments. The results are unreliable for comparing one state to other states.

The federal government has mandated programs without having a uniform testing program to see if standards have been met. They have left that important task up to each state. The results will only be good for each state and will not give a reliable accountability of the effectiveness of the programs nationwide.

There is no reliable national assessment of school programs in the United States. All states are allowed to do their own testing programs for their school curriculum. The data is only valid within that state. Thus far state tests have not helped to improve schools. Huge sums of money have been wasted on state tests that give the public no information on how schools compare with other schools nationally.[42]

There is an overwhelming demand to come up with an evaluation system of school education that will inform the public on how well students are being educated nationally. "New tests must provide accurate, reliable information to hold schools accountable. We need reliable information about student outcomes. Any proposed national examination must be a part of a broader plan that also integrates objectives, standards, teaching, assessments, and accountability," says Lynn Davey, author of *The Case for a National Testing System*.[43]

Such a system will cost billions of dollars to create. The yearly costs for testing every grade in the USA is billions of dollars nationally and is of questionable value. Due to this enormous cost and the information it will supply, there has to be a better way to educate America's students. It has been recommended that testing be done just three times instead of every year -- "once in elementary, middle and high school."[44]

No Child Left Behind

The federal government came out with an education plan (NCLB) that would set up goals that were to be met by 2014 and resulted with school districts getting huge amounts of money that met the goals of the program. The core of NCLB was mandatory testing. One thing about basing funding or teacher bonuses on test scores, it encourages cheating when goals are not met.[45,46]

Schools in Atlanta, Baltimore, Chicago, Michigan and Washington, D.C., have had cheating problems, but none involved law enforcement except Atlanta. The matter of fraud came to light when *The Atlanta Journal-Constitution* reported that some of the scores were statistically improbable.[47] The state released audits of test results after the newspaper published its analysis. U.S. Education Secretary Arne Duncan said the feds were looking at cheating in Atlanta Schools. Atlanta test cheating scandal was the nation's largest with 178 educators named in state investigation of widespread improprieties on standardized tests as far back as 2001.

State investigators revealed on July 5, 2011, that educators at nearly half of the districts 100 schools had changed answers on tests or given answers to students. The tests are used to measure whether districts are meeting federal benchmarks under NCLB law, and schools can receive thousands of dollars a year for improved scores. Atlanta school district had to return $363K to the federal government.

In Washington, D.C., test results for three schools have been tossed out over proven cases of cheating. The city's inspector general began investigating after *USA Today* reported that more than 100 D.C. Schools had unusually high rates of erasures on exams between 2008 and 2010.[48]

Changing students' answers to tests is no way to meet federal and/or state guidelines. Administrative pressure to meet goals is not sufficient to achieve the desired rise in national testing for the program. Education is being turned into a program to prepare students for state testing and not giving them the tools with which to be successful in learning basic subjects that will result in a foundation for students to become independent learners. It is time to get back to the elementary schools and have them adequately prepare students to become successful in middle and high schools so they will be able to go on to higher education and prepare themselves for the vocations they choose.

When federal government and business get together to set the course for education in America, we have a political and business team that does not have interests of students at heart. It is time to allow educators to set the goals and programs that will be just and fair for all students to get the best education that is available to them.

More and more teachers are required to 'teach the tests' in order for schools to get better test scores. Let's do away with state testing. It is costly and of questionable value. The use of multiple-choice tests is no true indicator of what students know. The USA is the only industrial nation in the world that uses this type of test to indicate student performance.[49] What makes it a waste of time, effort and money is the test score results cannot be used nationwide to let the public know how one state compares to other states. For this to happen every state must take the same test.

The major problem with NCLB testing is that every state can choose their own type of tests. Because testing is left up to states, there is no way to compare the effectiveness of one state's scores over other states. NCLB standards are not realistic. How can one state be compared with others? No state can meet the standard by 2014. State after state has petitioned to have waivers granted from the standards.[50]

New York States' Regent level, college preparation program

For years New York state had a Regents level track for high school students to earn a "college entrance diploma" at the end of their high school education. It was an optional choice. New York now has a requirement, that more students be enrolled in a Regents level, college preparatory program regardless of their future plans. Prior to 2000, there were student choices as to what track one would choose.

With the requirement of the Regents level college preparation program, students were under Regents' diploma track or some other track. Many students were under special education. One school district's 2007-2008 school year instructional budget expenses were: general education per pupil, $10,654, special education per pupil, $54,345. "If 24 students were kept out of special education, it could mean a savings of one million dollars every year."[51]

If states had a State Department Diploma for college level tract, technical and/or other tracks which indicated that students satisfactorily completed an approved four year high school course, it would qualify them for entrance into a higher level of education in their chosen fields whether in colleges, technical schools or other institutions. It would be a great encouragement for students to enter a track and complete the course to get such a diploma at high school graduation.

Here is an example of a College Entrance Diploma awarded in 1950. "The University of the State of New York Education Department be it known that (name of student) having satisfactorily passed examinations in English four years, science three years, intermediate algebra, plane geometry and American history and having submitted evidence of the satisfactory completion of an approved four year course in the (school name) is thereby entitled to this COLLEGE ENTRANCE DIPLOMA in witness whereof the Regents issue this diploma under the seal of the University, at Albany, in the (month/year/series number) Signed by Principal and Associate Commissioner of Education."[52]

Schools should work together to get a high school diploma program approved that would prepare students for entrance into higher education that would advance their education in chosen fields. The high schools would give the students the courses that met the basic requirements for a college entrance diploma.

Effectiveness of Nationwide Education in Schools

There are fifty states and no two states have the same educational basis for assessing how students perform on state tests compared to other states. There is a listing of fifty state's schools and their ratings. It's like looking at apples and oranges and comparing them according to likeness. With no one national standard, how can one rank them? With everyone wanting to know the comparisons of schools in different states, how can one make comparisons when there is no uniform standard? Get national tests on subjects that can be used to indicate how effective education is comparing one state with other states in language arts, mathematics, social studies and science.

SECTION TWO
OVERVIEW OF SOME PROBLEMS IN ELEMENTARY SCHOOLS
(CHAPTERS 5–9)

CHAPTER 5

SOME MAJOR PROBLEMS THAT MAY EXIST IN ELEMENTARY SCHOOLS

Some of the possible major problems which are introduced here can be easily changed if teachers and administrators are conscious of them before starting the new school year. One or more of the problems addressed may be a part of the overall problems with education today. No effort has been made to place each problem in the order of importance. The purpose is to identify some of the problems that may exist and propose a better way to educate students without causing discrimination. It is putting all students on the same level and treating each one as special. They need to be in an environment where they are accepted and respected.

Social Promotion

Some students are given social promotions every year with no plans to correct gaps in learning by placing them above their instructional levels in language arts and mathematics. These students have not met academic standards for the next year and their educational needs are not being addressed in order to remove the gaps. They move up to the next grade unprepared to adequately do the work. As this takes place year after year, they become less prepared to do the academic work. School does not become a positive place for them. If they reach grade twelve, their education is incomplete. These students may leave school without the skills for higher education or to earn livable wages. Some require five years in high school to graduate.[53] "Research findings indicate that, overall, neither social promotion nor retention offers lasting advantages nor leads to high performance."[54] Perhaps a better use of instructional time than to prepare students to take state tests that reveal that some students are not ready for life after school is to make sure students are ready for grade level work.

Teachers Preparing Students for Mandated Tests

National testing is a good indicator for giving the results of student achievement. These tests are needed and are indicators of how well students are doing in school. But to have state tests that show how students are doing in the programs falls far short of giving a true picture when students cannot read on grade level and do not know basic mathematics well enough to handle middle and high school math. The pressure is on schools to show that students are learning better now than in the past. There are better ways to use educational time instead of for state testing. The results of state mandated testing are a loss of teaching time, undermining creativity and thinking, narrowing the curriculum, teaching the tests, obscuring real achievement gaps, stress on students, loss of talented teachers and high financial costs.[55]

Multiple Choice (A, B, C, or D) Type of Tests

For sure, this type of test is quickly scored, but what does this indicate about the students' knowledge? They know the answers, or they are good at guessing. There are students who have trouble reading, who just go down the list of questions and mark a letter for each question. Usually these are poor students and finish early. It is this type of student who brings down the test scores for a school. There are better types of tests to give than multiple-choice tests. A better way is to give tests where the students have to fill in blanks or tell all they know about a subject. Yes, these types of tests take more time to score, but give teachers, schools and parents a more accurate indicator of what the students know.

Discrimination Of Students

Historically schools used three types of homerooms on grade level, if they had enough students. There were homerooms for below average, average, and above average students. This practice may still exist in some schools. Students quickly know what levels they are in. The group in the below average are identified by the rooms in which they are placed and are not being treated fairly in these settings. Many times students whose language is not English or are from low income homes end up in the below-average group. There is a better nondiscriminatory way to avoid identifying student differences then in room placement.

There Are Laws About School But Not Teaching

There are no laws that teachers must teach students how to read or know mathematics. There are laws about how many school days in a school year, the number of fire and storm drills that must be carried out during a school year and what holidays are to be observed just to name a few. Parents want their children to be taught how to read and to know basic mathematics among other things that are taught in the elementary schools. If a teacher is making success unavoidable for students, that teacher cares for the students' needs.

Teacher's Lounge Converstion Topics

When teachers unload their classroom frustrations relating to one or more of their students, they are planting thoughts in the minds of other teachers who may have one of those students in their classroom in the future.

Preconceived notions about students before one has an opportunity to fairly evaluate those students are not the way students are to be characterized. It is understandable that teachers get frustrated, but it should never be at the student's expense. There are positive ways to talk about students in the teachers' lounge. Teachers need to speak wisely and not negatively about their students. Could teachers want the staff to feel sorry for them because so and so is in their rooms?

Many times home visits can open the eyes of teachers in knowing more about the home situations and how they can better help and understand the students. In these cases, two teachers should go to the home, and only the student's teacher asks the questions.

Home visits also indicate to a parent or parents that teachers really care about how well their students are doing in school. Visits should not be only when there is a problem but also to report how well a student is doing.

If there are other students in the same area, the teacher can visit them. Parents talk with neighbors, and this lets them know that their students are just as important to you as the first parents visited.

Some Students Should Not Take State Tests

Students in special education classes should be exempted from taking that state test if their Individual Education Plan (IEP) does not include taking state tests. Also students who are below grade level in reading or cannot read English well enough should not have to take the test. If they do take the test, one who can read should help them if necessary – not to give answers but to make sure they know the questions.

Not Teaching Every Student In The Classrooms

Regarding socially promoted students, some may feel they do not have the time to teach these students at their instructional levels so they are ignored as long as they do not disrupt the class. These students are passed each year in order to stay up with their peers. There is no emphasis or effort put forth to catch these students up in their learning.

Spending More Time With One Group Of Students

Some teachers, having top and bottom level students in the classroom, may spend more instructional time with low achieving students to bring their low students up. On the other hand, another teacher with the same composition may spend more instructional time with their high level students than with their lower level students. This is called the Peter or Paul method. It is spending more time with one group at the expense of the other groups. This can happen when teachers have too many different levels to teach. Is it fair to ignore one group of students?

When teachers have three groups to teach, each group gets at the most one third of the class period for instruction on their levels. Teachers who have more levels to teach in a class may have less time with each group. This is depriving the most needy students of adequate instructional time each day. It is not fair to the needy students.

Also thinking that seatwork to one group instead of instructional time is a good way to keep groups busy while spending instructional time with the favored or needy group is discriminatory. This method could work the other way. Spending more time with the advanced students at the expense of the poor students also may result. The problem is caused when teachers have an impossible situation – having more levels present than there is time to adequately teach each group.

Teachers With Many Levels Of Preparation A Day

For example, a teacher has twenty-five students in a class. The subject being taught has students on six different levels. No teacher can successfully teach six different levels of reading in one day in one class period. There is just not that much time in one class period to teach six different levels of reading. The problem is caused by social promotion. Teachers are also receiving students who are not prepared for the present grade. The AUG Plan has the answer to this problem.

Filling Homerooms Without Placement Plans

Having homerooms like in the past where there were three levels per grade—below average, average, and above average—causes discrimination of students. Not having a placement plan also causes major problems for the administrator and teachers.

Placing students with no plan in mind can result in having several students with the same first name in the same room. It can also cause an imbalance of sexes, races, learning levels in language arts and/or mathematics. These are a few problems that are caused by not having a plan. There must be a reasonable way of placing students that is not discriminatory.

Practice Of Starting New Year With New Books

Not every teacher finishes language arts and basic mathematics book for the school year. Those students miss very important subject matter. When the next school year begins, new books are issued. Eventually, gaps that are found and increase are to the disadvantage of students.

Teachers who are not covering grade level material by the end of the year are not treating students fairly. Planning the teaching of the curriculum for all teachers is expected. The students deserve it. The school should require it. Parents have a right to expect it. There is a better way to overcome this problem: plan the teaching year in such a way for the important textbook material to be covered.

Teach Students How To Get Along With Others

Schools should teach every student how to get along with everyone and work together for the common good. There is no better place to teach respect for self and others than in a heterogeneous homeroom. Bullying is a major problem in many schools, even to the point of causing death of students. All homerooms should have students representing the whole community. What better place is there to teach respect and consideration for others than in a heterogeneous homeroom?

Plans To Make Grade Level Homerooms Different

Any effort to make one grade level homeroom different from the others is not the American way. That is how to promote educational discrimination.

Students on grade level should be placed in homerooms that are basically the same as the other homerooms, which represent the composition of the community. Everything possible has been done to make students successful, positive and feeling special in a homeroom where they are able to assist those who have not mastered a skill or use their strengths to help their group excel in learning.

If any of these problems exist in the elementary school, every effort should be made to correct them. The learning environment should be the safest for educating students.

Section 2

CHAPTER 6

SOME CAUSES OF DISCIPLINE PROBLEMS

Frustration and boredom may cause disruptions

Bored and frustrated students can cause disruption and discipline problems in the classrooms and homerooms. However, with students being educated on their instructional levels, there will be less frustrations. When all students have success and are actively involved with their groups, the causes for discipline are greatly reduced.

In the present day's situation, when students are placed with those who are below grade, on grade and above grade levels in the same classroom, there is bound to be frustration and boredom. Those who are on grade level do not cause many problems. The below grade level students are the ones who may be frustrated because they do not know the material. These students many times are not going to let it be known to their peers that they do not know the answers if called upon to respond. Those who are above grade level may be the ones who are bored because they already know the material. These students, instead of sitting quietly and paying attention, find something else to do which disrupts the class. They may be looking out the window, getting out of their seats or any number of other disruptive actions. When disruptions happen, they are taking valuable learning time away from all the students.

No forethought in placing students in homerooms

When there are no standards or guidelines to go by, there is always the probability that some disruptions are going to happen. Sometimes disruption problems occur by students' interactions. Having former teachers indicating what students should not be placed together will reduce discipline problems in the new school year.

Teachers can be aware of who are causing disruptions and where they are sitting in the room. For students who are causing disruptions with students around them, the teacher can move the student to another seat, preferably near the teacher's desk.

There have been many problems with students who are sitting at the back of the room. The teacher should ask how well students can see the board or hear the teacher. Sometime students need glasses and no one has recognized it. A student making poor grades and sitting away from the board may have need of glasses or be hard of hearing which may be another cause of disruptions.

School lockdowns

With the crimes that are being carried out in and near schools, it has become necessary to have school lockdowns. This policy has come about because of Columbine School where students were sent out and were killed by a sniper. Today students are not allowed to leave their rooms if there is an emergency, such as a bomb threat, a stranger in the school, an emergency outside of the school, etc. Teachers need to be prepared with plans to keep students from worrying or being over anxious due to the unknown. Sometimes the lockdowns can last for hours which causes major room disruptions and stops the learning process. Teachers can make special plans of what to do to keep the students' minds occupied. Some suggestions are showing an appropriate film, keeping their minds active in a learning experience, have students share a positive experience they have had, where they went on vacation, places they visited or some hands-on activity in the classroom. It is good to keep them away from the windows and follow plans the school has in place if lockdowns are taking place.

Fire, tornado, hurricane drills

Schools are mandated by law to have several kinds of drills throughout the school year. According to the law, fire drills particularity must be held monthly during the school year. Hurricane and tornado drills are scheduled about twice during the fall season. It is extremely important that students' behavior is appropriate. Usually at the beginning of the school year there are students new to the school and may not know how to behave in these drills. Teachers usually have the students prepared for such drills. However, there are times when unacceptable behavior may be shown. It may be good to let those students be with the teachers until they learn acceptable behavior. When they learn the right behavior, they can go to their usual place in line during such drills.

Unprepared teacher

Whenever a teacher comes to class unprepared, there will always be students who will detect that and take advantage of the situation and cause disruptions. The students will find ways to occupy their time while the teacher struggles to present the lesson. Then the teacher will have the added difficulty of regaining the students' attention.

Unusual things that happen outside of the classroom

There are distractions that happen outside the classroom, in the hall or outside the building that cause disruptions. It may be a loud noise and someone will try to run to the door or look out the window to see what is happening. With the situations as they are today, it is urgent that students be told never to go to the door or windows under any situation. As outside noises are distractions and may cause disruptions, students should be cautioned not to ever get out of their seats to check them out. The teacher can step to the door and look out the window, without opening the door or to the window and look outside, if that is necessary.

Students who cause disruption in the class

The teacher can separate the students by placing them apart where they will not be close enough to start another disruption. Then the parents should be informed about what happened and encouraged to share ideas about what the student may do to improve the situation.

The physical layout of the room

The classroom conditions and arrangements are key elements to check to insure that no discipline problems are caused by the room environment. The room temperature being too hot or cold, the sun shining in student's eyes or the light not being adequate are things to check and keep in mind when disruptions may be caused by one of these conditions.

Other causes of disruptions

Bullying This behavior is a big problem in many schools. Every effort should be taken in the homeroom to provide experiences that will help to overcome this situation. Causes are many. Sometimes the bully is the victim of bullying in the home, school or community. The one way to stop it is not to tolerate the practice.

Stealing One way to correct this is to have affordable school uniforms. If a student does not have the funds to purchase them, the school could have a project to raise funds for this purpose or an organization in the community could do this. Having school uniforms would remove the pressure of keeping up with the fads.

Putting others down Classes could have a weekly or monthly award for the student who was the most thoughtful and helpful. It would be setting a positive goal for the whole class.

Gangs In the heterogeneous, integrated homeroom, students can model the behavior they want to have in their community—caring about each other, getting along, working in harmony, helping one another, solving problems together and modeling cooperation.

Talking while the teacher or someone else is speaking Warn talkers to stop talking when others are talking. If that does not work, separate talkers.

Passing notes Have a rule that passing notes is unacceptable during class is a way to control this problem. Many times having simple rules that address these matters posted will remind students of acceptable behavior.

Physical problems There may be many physical problems such as - not being able to see or hear the teacher, needing reading glasses, being uncomfortable in the desk or having an obstruction between the teacher and student. Such situations should be addressed as they arise.

CHAPTER 7

SELF-CONCEPT AND SELF-ESTEEM
AND WHY THEY'RE IMPORTANT

The testing of self-concept of public school students on national tests showed that 50% scored below 50 percentile. The self-concept of public school students is significantly low. It is very interesting to look at the self-concept of students. Teachers need to know how important this is in helping students to feel good about themselves in order for them to do well in academics.

One year the author was a teacher in an emotionally handicapped self-contained class of twelve students from grades 3 through 5. It did not take long to find out that until they felt good about themselves, they could not be taught. As students' self-concept improved, their schoolwork improved. At the end of the school year, over half of the class were staffed back to their grade level and did not require a self-contained class setting. Their positive self-concept made the difference in the class.

When it comes to self-concept, one has to know what it is in order to help the students. Suppose students get all A's, the self-concept is very high. If a student keeps getting failing grades, the self-concept will be entirely different. When students are placed in settings that are above their instructional levels in language arts and basic mathematics, their self-concept will be lowered. Now if teachers make success unavoidable for all students, what will it do for the self-concept? All students will experience success and feel good about themselves. It takes a teacher who believes all students can be successful and does not accept less from each student that makes the difference in reference to improving self-concept.

Development of Academic Self-Concept

Academic Self-Concept (ASC) develops about ages 7-8, when students are in second or third grades.[56] This is when they begin evaluating their own ASC by comparing themselves to their peers. The majority of students will be reading on grade level by the end of third grade. "If the trend holds true 6.6 million low-income children in the birth to age 8 group are at risk of failing to graduate from high school on time...."[57] Social promotion is doing a disservice to these students because their needs in language arts and basic mathematics are not being met in the receiving grades. "Failure to read proficiently is linked to higher rate of school dropouts which suppresses individual earning potential as well as the nation's competitiveness and general productivity."[58]

The major causes of low self-esteem in elementary schools are students who are not reading on grade level and/or have not mastered basic mathematics.

What is happening in schools today? Students are being promoted without academic achievement and end up at the bottom of their classes during their remaining school years. For this reason alone, the elementary schools need to have an instructional plan that will allow students to be promoted and at the same time be taught language arts and basic mathematics on their instructional levels. This way almost all of the students will enter middle school on their grade level. A few students may not be on grade level by the end of fifth grade. In that case, middle school can begin at their instructional levels to get them on grade levels in language arts and/or basic mathematics.

Self-concept and self-esteem

These concepts are not the same thing. Self-concept is the knowing side of knowledge about self. Self-esteem is the feeling side.

Teachers must be on the alert what they say about students and what they allow others to say about students. Teachers should model respect for others and encourage students to do the same. There are no two students exactly the same. Each one is special and of value. Bullying and put downs should not be allowed to happen in school. Schools should seek to build good self-concepts in all students.

Parents must help their children to develop good self-concepts. Children need to be told that they are loved and are important to every member of the family. Children learn who they are by the way others treat them. The golden rule reminds people to…"do to others what you would have them do to you." [59]

Self-esteem is internal. It is how one feels about self. Everyone can build one's self-esteem by saying positive things and building one another up by what they do for them. For teachers, making success unavoidable for all students builds their self-esteem.

Parents and teachers have great input in helping students develop outstanding self-concept and self-esteem. Setting a good example for others to follow is a great way for that to begin.

Why is this so important

It is extremely important because both parents and teachers play important roles in helping to mold students' lives in making them outstanding citizens. But it does not stop there. Fellow students and everyone they meet have an influence either for good or bad on these young lives.

From 1970-1990 suicides tripled among children 5-14. In the age range 10-14, it is the third leading killer of children.[60] Bullying is the main cause in most cases.

In July, 2012, a 13-year old youth in Japan was bullied by students and committed suicide.[61] Teachers as well as students were witnesses to the bullying and did nothing but laugh at it. No one should ever allow bullying to take place.

Life is precious. Everyone is one of a kind. Life should be protected and not destroyed. Remember, everybody is loved by God. One's self-concept must be respected and every endeavor must be to increase one's self-worth.

Impact of reading/language arts and basic mathematics on self

The secret in educating students on their instructional levels in reading/language arts and mathematics is to build their self-esteem and self-concept to the place where they will be able to handle all future learning with success. This can only happen when reading/language arts is taught in every elementary grade at the same time. Students then can go to the teachers who are teaching their levels.

This must also be done for basic mathematics, where all teachers are teaching the subject at the same time. The students go to the teachers who are teaching their levels. This way, for foundational subjects, no gaps will occur in learning, and students will move at their own rate of learning. This can be done effectively in the elementary schools at no additional cost for staff. It is just a matter of scheduling.

Students not on grade level and self-concept

Students who are on grade level have good self-concepts regarding school work. However, there may be problems outside of the school that teachers never know about that can cause poor self-concepts. Many teachers know of teachers that have destroyed the self-concepts of students. What is so sad about this is that these students have never recovered from the way they were treated by teachers, parents or students.

One student had to repeat an elementary grade three times. No one sought to help the student. The scars are visible even today after almost thirty years. This type of teacher should never be allowed in the classroom, whether in the public, private or any other school. The classroom should be the place where every teacher makes all students feel good about themselves. Bullying should not be tolerated in any school setting. All this has to do with self-concept. The teacher is in the best place to protect self-concepts by stopping behavior that tears down one's self-concept.

Conclusion

One's self-concept is critical. Teachers must do all they can to discourage any effort by a teacher, parent or student to tear down one's self-concept. There have been many studies conducted to research a student's self-concept. Teachers need to be aware and know how to handle situations where students are being put down. The news reports contain far too many student suicides. It is a major problem. Teachers are in a position to build a good self-concept and strive for it in the life of each student. This behavior should be a goal in every class.

Educators are mandated by law to report any situation where child abuse is suspected by students, parents or teachers. They should do all they can to protect the well-being of every child. Getting students on grade level in language arts and basic mathematics has everything to do in increasing one's self-concept. Their self-concepts must be positive.

CHAPTER 8

SOCIAL PROMOTION AND ABILITY GROUPING OF STUDENTS

Social promotion is the practice of promoting a student from one grade level to the next on the basis of age rather than academic achievement.[62] Social promotion has been around a long time. There are a number of school districts which have practiced it, and then abandoned it, and then have taken it up again. A few examples of this are New York City schools[63] and Los Angeles schools.[64] The problems of social promotion will be with education until someone comes up with a better plan for its removal. "It's plausible that holding kids back would be good. But the evidence is overwhelming that it's very harmful...."[65]

As long as teachers are allowed to teach subjects without teaching students, the problems will always exist. When social promotion is practiced, someone has failed to adequately prepare students for the next higher grades.

To make the situation even worse, the receiving teachers pass students up to the next grades when achievement goals still have not been met. Wherein do the problems lie? Is it with the teachers or with the students? Is it with schools or with the district boards?

• Follow these scenarios: First, students find out they do not have to do the work to be promoted. Just attend class and at the end of the year promotion is sure. With a few students, this is an easy way out. Studying school material is hard work, so just do not do it. It is the student's fault.

• Scenario two. The teacher accepts non-participation and does not urge the students to do the work. Just do not disturb the class, and you will be promoted. It is the teacher's fault.

• Scenario three. The teacher does not get the students up to grade level before the year is over. Let the receiving teachers next year deal with the situation; it is now their problem.

This practice is totally unfair for the receiving teachers. The problems of below-grade-level students moving up to the next grades continues all the way through high school. That is where we are now. The low test scores reveal the schools' failure to adequately educate all students in these two subjects.

It is impossible for teachers to do a successful job teaching students language arts and/or basic mathematics when they have so many different levels to prepare for each day in these subjects. It is also not fair to students when their instructional time is drastically shortened because the teacher is teaching so many different groups during the period.

• Scenario four. Teachers cannot be held responsible for teaching language arts and basic mathematics to such a wide range of instructional levels when the AUG Plan is the solution. The curriculum coordinator or administrator who sets up the placement of students can do it according to the Plan. It makes provision for students to be taught language arts and basic mathematics on their instructional levels.

The problems in the past were that social promotion had no plan to assist students to make up what they missed in the sending grade. Each passing year, the gaps grew greater, and the students were not able to handle the grade level work in their promoted grades. Whose fault was it? It is the fault of the educational system. Who suffers the most within these systems – the students? What a price students have to pay when the emphasis was on passing state tests, but not on teacher educating students in reading and basic mathematics in the elementary schools.

There are at least three reasons why social promotion is practiced.

• One reason for social promotion may be athletics. Why retain students when the athletic programs will suffer. The bigger athletes are needed in the high schools' programs. If students are retained, they will be old enough for the athletic competition before they reach high school. But they cannot be involved in high school sports because they have not reached ninth grade.

• A second reason for social promotion was one's self-concept. It is not good for students to be two or more years older in age in a class and having younger students with more knowledge then they in the same room. The psychological and social well-being of the students are at stake. If they are retained, it may be that the parents wanted the student held back for a year due to immaturity, and the next year the student would not be at the bottom of the class. If that is the reason, those students may feel that is because they failed the grade.

It may be better in this case to hold the students out of school one year or have them spend another year in kindergarten before starting school instead of having them repeat the grade. This way, instead of beginning the year at the bottom of the class, they may be average or above average students their first year.

If it is for academic reasons, it is known that they flunked the grade and is almost always academically and emotionally harmful to the students. It generally does not lead to sustained academic improvement, lowers students' self-esteem and leads to dropping out of school. Parents are told, "Never mind the academics, their social needs are greater."[66] This mind set is not in the best educational needs of the socially promoted students. They are being placed above grade level in classes and given an unfair educational setting. They were at the bottom in the sending grade and end up at the bottom in the receiving grade.

• A third reasons given for social promotion were "fear that high failure rates would reflect poorly on the school personnel, pressure exerted by principal and parents to promote unready students, knowledge that retention is ineffective and the absence or insufficiency of effective educations alternatives to social promotion."[67]

Social promotion is not needed above the elementary grades and, in fact, Mayor Michael Bloomberg of New York said, "social promotion will end in the fifth grade."

"School officials are struggling with how to eliminate social promotion and at the same time provide manageable cost-efficient programs that promote positive student achievement."[68]

According to the AUG Plan, no student should fail in the elementary schools. All students should be promoted every year. This is said with the understanding that their academic needs in language arts and basic mathematics will be met according to the AUG Plan in homogeneous classrooms where students are put with other students on their same levels.

Ability Grouping

"Ability grouping...is the practice of grouping children according to their talents in the classroom.... At the elementary school level...kids are divided into the Bluebirds and Redbirds.... Labels that stay with them as they move from grade to grade.[69] Many say this practice limits the cultural and interracial respect. In the past, this concept resulted in segregation of races and isolating minority students in below average settings. The practice was not one that treated everyone with dignity and respect. It discriminated against both the below and above-average students, in addition to race and culture.

The later ability grouping is introduced into a school system, say fourth or fifth grades, the more questions will be raised about its purpose. Why has it taken so long to practice ability grouping without the reasons that were first used to practice it? With all of the problems in education, ability grouping should not be a problem under the AUG Plan. Ability grouping places all students on the same levels in homogeneous classrooms for two periods for language arts and one period for basic mathematics each day, a total of three periods.

All other subjects (science, social studies, health, physical education, music and art) are taught in heterogeneous homerooms on grade level in the elementary school. Using the AUG Plan, all homogeneous classes in the homogeneous classrooms have the same instructional composition. In the past, other combinations were used because educators did not have an organizational plan that would justly and fairly address students' educational needs relating to their instructional levels. These mistakes of the past are not repeated in the AUG Plan.

In conclusion, social promotion resulted in major problems. No one teacher was able to teach to the needs of below-average, average and above-average students in the homeroom during the teaching of language arts and mathematics; except for, science, social studies, health, music, art and physical education, which are all taught on grade level.

As a result, there was a large outcry against using ability grouping as a way to educate students in many schools because of its misuse in the past.[70] Ability grouping does have an important place in teaching some subjects, but not in having students together all day for all subjects.

After looking at much of the findings of research, there is a solution that is in the best interest of every student involved. It is the answer to the educational, physical, psychological and social issues—with the best interests of the students in mind. It is contained in the AUG Plan.

CHAPTER 9

TEACHERS' ATTITUDES, PREPARATIONS ADVANAGES AND STUDENTS' ADVANTAGES IN CLASSROOMS AND HOMEROOMS

Teachers' Attitudes

Attitudes are contagious. They can be caught. Teachers who teach subjects and do not believe it is important for students to master the material may be a cause for students being retained.

Retention is the ability to remember what was taught, apply what was learned, and change previous behavior. One can know students have learned when behavior changes. If there is no change in behavior, it is difficult to know if students have learned.

The teachers' attitudes about students, their preparation for teaching language arts and basic mathematics, and their important other preparations are all factors that need to be considered when placing students with teachers in classes. It is possible to create an impossible task for teachers if consideration is not given to help them have the best possible conditions for teaching successfully.

Teachers' Preparations for Language Arts and Basic Mathematics

Language Arts

In the regular heterogeneous homerooms in a K–5 school, the number of reading levels could be up to eight, for grades 2–5. It is impossible for one teacher to teach more than three different reading levels in one classroom during a two–period class. That would require many different reading preparations for every class day. It cannot be humanly done along with the other daily subject preparations.

Now if an elementary school had every teacher teaching language arts at the same time, the "many different reading levels" in a homogeneous classroom would be solved. Every teacher would have only one level to prepare for each day. The students would go to the homogeneous classrooms where the teachers were teaching their level with no more than three touching units during the reading period in each classroom. All students would advance to the next levels when 80% mastery was achieved on each unit of a level.

For the sight words, there are five levels, and each level must be mastered at 100%. There are 220 words on the Dolch Sight Word List which can be purchased at school supply stores or magazine stands. The list and numbers of words are: Pre-primer 40, Primer 52, Grade One 41, grade two 46 and grade three 41.[71] When students have mastered the list for each level, they have achieved reading words on their level that are learned only through memorization.

Basic Mathematics

In the regular heterogeneous homerooms, there will be different levels of basic mathematics. With 25-30 students in a homeroom, it is difficult for one teacher to teach all students on their instructional levels.

If all grades were teaching mathematics at the same time, the students would be taught on their instructional levels in homogeneous classrooms by going to teachers who were teaching their levels. Students would advance to the next units upon 80% mastery for each unit. The goal is to have the elementary students master the basic concepts of mathematics before they leave each one – counting, addition, subtraction, multiplication, division, measurement and fractions. If students do not know how to count they will have problems with addition and so on with each math concept taught in the elementary school. Further, if students do not master basic mathematics, they will have major problems with all future maths in both middle and high schools.

There are many advantages of teaching language arts at the same time for all grades and teaching basic mathematics at the same time for all grades. When students can go to the teachers who are teaching their instructional levels in these subjects, no teacher has an impossible teaching environment. All students in every classroom are with students on their own levels. There are only average students within all classrooms for instruction in the elementary school. It is within the teachers' power to teach in a way to make success unavoidable for all students in the classrooms.

Teacher's Advantages in teaching reading and basic mathematics in homogeneous classrooms instead of heterogeneous homerooms

The greatest advantage is no teacher will have to teach students who are below-grade level, on grade level or above-grade level in language arts and basic mathematics in their heterogeneous homerooms. All students will go to the teacher who is teaching their instructural levels in homogeneous classrooms.

Teachers will have fewer levels to teach each day in these classes. Instead of having to teach many units and/or levels, they will only teach touching units and/or levels. Each year they can teach the same levels and new students will be in their classes, depending on their instructional units and/or levels.

The teachers will have fewer language arts units to prepare for each day. They will have fewer basic mathematics preparations for each day. All students will be taught on their instructional levels and will master language arts and basic mathematics before moving on to the next units in the classrooms. This will make success unavoidable for all students.

Teachers will not have below-grade level or above-grade level students in their classrooms. All students will get the benefit of 100% of instructional time and be on the same instructional units and/or levels.

This educational plan is favored by many frustrated teachers. No teacher will be overwhelmed in the homeroom having to face an impossible teaching situation where students are on many different levels in language arts and basic mathematics.

Other major advantages are that teachers can use students who have mastered a skill to assist students who are having difficulty with a concept. Teachers also have the advantage of having students hear the instruction that is going on while the other units are being taught to groups two and three. Because the instruction is on touching levels, every student benefits from what is said in the classroom.

In summary, this method of teaching students these subjects benefits all students. It corrects the problems of having students leaving fifth grade without being on grade level in language arts and not having mastered basics of mathematics. There may be some students that leave fifth grade without reading on grade level and/or mastering the basics of mathematics. If this happens, then the middle schools have to reach these students where they are and teach them on their instructional levels in these subjects. If there are some students who enter high school and are not reading on grade level or have not mastered basic mathematics, the high schools should instruct them on their instructional levels in order for them to graduate having mastered these subjects.

Students' Advantages in Heterogeneous Homerooms

All subjects in the heterogeneous homerooms are taught on grade level. The subjects taught in homerooms are science, social studies, health, music, art and physical education. In the homerooms, there will be students below-grade level, on-grade level and above-grade level. All grade level students will be taught grade level subjects.

By forming groups within all homerooms, made up of all levels of language arts and basic mathematics, there will be students who have mastered language arts and basic mathematics who will be able to help students who may yet have not yet mastered those skills within their groups.

Because language arts and basic mathematics are not necessary in order to be successful in the homerooms, students who are below grade level in these subjects can learn grade level subjects.

Further, the present day heterogeneous homeroom situations are unfair to the below-grade level and above-grade level students in both language arts and basic mathematics because no teacher can properly teach all levels present during the same language arts and/or mathematics periods if taught in homerooms.

There are many advantages to this classroom situation. All students are on similar levels. There are no smarter or dumber students in class with them. When touching levels are being taught in both subjects, students have many advantages. For example, in language arts or mathematics, students who are on similar units can benefit by hearing the teacher teaching the students in units before their unit or that follow their unit. Also students who have mastered a unit can help students who are having a problem with a concept in a unit they have mastered. Much reinforcement can take place in this classroom setting.

Students' Advantages in Homogeneous Classrooms

The advantages for students are fourfold.

• First, all students will be taught beginning on their instructional levels in language arts and basic mathematics in homogeneous classrooms. Very few students will leave fifth grade not reading on grade level or mastering basic mathematics.

• Secondly, if any student is below grade level by the end of fifth grade in these two subjects, the middle school will instruct the students on their instructional level until they are on grade level. These classes end when the student masters the skills and is on grade level.

• Thirdly, no students will be placed below or above their instructional levels; that means, all students are "average" in the classroom. No instructional time will be taken from them in order to teach unrelated levels. Success is unavoidable in this setting.

• Fourthly, students who are on many different levels in reading and basic mathematics will be taught on their instructional levels only in homogeneous classrooms that are teaching their level. This is arranged to give the elementary schools time to get students on grade level in language arts and basic mathematics before they advance to middle school.

• It is the purpose of the AUG Plan to make the learning environment ideal for each student. The classroom and homeroom organization concepts are providing the best solution for the problems in the elementary schools where students are not on grade level in language arts and basic mathematics.

The AUG Plan solves two great elementary school problems. First, in language arts and basic mathematics, all students are taught on their instructional levels in homogeneous classrooms. For the students that results in all students being in a class where everyone is on the same level. They are all average students. There are no below or above-level students present to take instructional time away from them.

Secondly, all students in the heterogeneous homerooms are being taught grade level subjects in an environment where the emphasis is on group learning. Everyone in the group has something to offer to make the group successful. Every effort has been made to have an excellent learning environment where everyone can learn together. It is fulfilling to see how this organizational plan results in improved self-concept and self-esteem not only for the students but also for teachers.

SECTION THREE
THE AUG PLAN
(CHAPTERS 10–14)

CHAPTER 10

THE AUG PLAN FOR THE ELEMENTARY SCHOOL

The AUG Plan for educating elementary students is an organizational plan to structure the learning environments so students will be successful in the elementary school subjects being taught. The plan calls for two major changes in the structure of the elementary schools.

• The first structural change is to teach science, social studies, health, physical education, music and art in homerooms.

• The second major structural change is to teach language arts and basic mathematics in classrooms. These are the most foundational subjects taught in the elementary school. Without them students cannot be successful in all future classes.

The administration, teachers, staff, students and textbooks of the school remain unchanged. The subjects taught do not change. However, these important changes will result in elementary school students going to middle school on grade level. The changes will also allow elementary schools to successfully achieve their goals of educating all students to perform well in all their future learning.

Forming Heterogeneous Homerooms

The first major change in the AUG Plan is placing students in heterogeneous homerooms. When there are only enough students for one homeroom, the placement of students has already been completed for that grade level. The goal is to have every homeroom on grade level just like the community. However, if there were enough students for other homerooms on-grade-level, the following steps are suggested:

• There are only seven factors for pre-school, kindergarten and first grade homeroom placement: grade level, name, address, sex, race, how students arrive at school, and disability.

• There are nine factors to use in placing students in homerooms for grades 2 through 5. They are: name, address, grade level, sex, race, reading level, mathematics level, how students arrive at school, and disability. Other factors may be added depending on each situation. For example, students who do not get along in the sending class, personality conflicts, or cliques may need to be placed in different rooms.

• In the kindergarten and first grade classes, all instruction is done in class. There is little movement outside of the room unless for physical education, or for students that have to go up a grade level for language arts and/or basic mathematics. Some students may go to second grade because of their instructional levels. Placement tests will reveal if they need to go up a grade for instruction. After instruction in language arts and/or basic mathematics, they will return to their grade level homerooms.

Factors in Forming Heterogeneous Homerooms

Grade level: The number of homerooms on a grade level depends on the number of students in that grade. If there were 75 students, there would be 3 homerooms based on 25 students per room. See chart in Chapter 14 for additional information on how many homerooms are needed according to the numbers of students.

Sex: There would be the same number of girls in each room and the same number of boys. Some rooms may have one more or less depending on how many of each sex were on grade level. No sex would be in isolation. There would always be a minimum of two girls or boys in a homeroom. Never only one. For example, if there were two girls on a grade level, they would be in the same homeroom.

Race: There would be the same number of students of each race by including girls and boys in every homeroom. No student of race would be in isolation. There would always be two of each race, if possible, in a room. If there were only two, they would be in the same homeroom. Gender does not apply in this category.

Reading: There would be the same number of above–average, average and below–average reading students in every homeroom.

Basic Mathematics: There would be the same number of above–average, average and below–average math students in every homeroom.

Disability: There may be mentally and/or physically challenged students mainstreamed and placed in homerooms based on their IEP's. Depending on their number, there should be only one in a room. If there were more than one, and it is not a handicapped class, whatever decision is made, it should always be in the best interest of the student.

Address: If this is necessary, place students from the same neighborhoods in different homerooms to minimize neighborhood problems being brought into the homeroom.

How students arrive at school: The thought is to separate students based on where they live. If there were a problem on the bus, in the neighborhood or in the carpool, it might follow into the homeroom. This is just looking ahead to where school discipline problems might occur.

First name: A homeroom should not have two students with the same first name in the same room. If there is only one homeroom on a grade level or a homeroom that ends up with two with the same first name, one may prefer to use a middle name for the school year. It would not be changed on the permanent record and would only be used during the present year. This would remove confusion caused by two or more students with the same first name.

Subjects To Be Taught In The Heterogeneous Homerooms In Grades One Through Five

It is extremely important how subjects are taught in the heterogeneous homerooms. **Subjects taught in heterogeneous homerooms by the teachers are all on-grade level** and may include science, social studies, health, physical education, music and art.

Some elementary schools are able to have specialists teach classes in art, music and physical education. These specialists teach their subjects in heterogeneous homerooms, or they may have their own classrooms for instruction to teach their subjects. In some instances where the school does not have these specialists, the teachers who are certified will teach these subjects to their homeroom.

Forming Groups Within The Heterogeneous Homerooms

The teacher can form five or six groups within the homeroom in teaching the grade level subjects. Each group should be formed on the same basis as the homeroom. The same number of low-average, average and above-average students in language arts and basic mathematics in each group. The average and above-average students could assist the students who are weak in areas that require reading and mathematics.

Some of the students may be strong in art, speaking, organizing or whatever is needed to complete a project. The purpose is to allow students to work together and add to the success of their group. Groups may be changed by the teacher every five or six weeks, depending on the subject matter. This will help students to develop working relationships within their group and learn how to cooperate with other students. Because the heterogeneous homerooms are exact replicas of the community, students can carry their working relationship experiences with others back into their communities.

The AUG Plan brings the community into the homeroom where students are learning to work together because they are a combination of every segment of the outside community—name, sex, race, below–average, average, and above-average in language arts and mathematics, coming to school by bus, car or walking, handicapped, and living in different areas of the school zone. All heterogeneous homerooms on every grade level have similar composition of students.

Forming Homogeneous Classrooms

Here is where the AUG Plan makes the most important change in correcting the main weaknesses of the present day elementary schools. The problem is that far too many students are leaving the elementary schools and going into the middle schools not reading on-grade-level and/or mastering basic mathematics.

This is caused because students were socially promoted without mastering language arts and basic mathematics. The receiving teachers cannot teach effectively the many levels in language arts and basic mathematics in their classrooms. Too many students leave their classes at the end of the year still not on grade level. Below–grade level students have almost an impossible task to get on–grade level after being socially promoted. The AUG Plan was conceived to treat all students fairly and to treat them so they feel good about themselves. One big advantage of the Plan is that students are in an organizational program where they feel good about themselves because they are in a school where they are successful.

The purpose of the elementary school is to prepare students for the middle and high schools in language arts and basic mathematics. For many students going to middle schools not having mastered language arts and basic mathematics, their success in middle and high school is never assured. If students have not mastered these basics, they may drop out of school.

Studies have shown that many students who were socially promoted with gaps in their learning, which were never filled, dropped out of school and some ended up in jail, all because they were not properly educated according to their instructional level.[72, 73] For more research on this serious situation, every teacher and administrator should read *Pygmalion In The Classroom* by Robert

Rosenthal and Lenore Jacobson to see what teacher expectation has to do with helping students to be successful in their education.[74]

Reasons For Forming Homogeneous Classrooms

The second major change relates to the two most important subjects which are taught in the elementary schools: language arts and basic mathematics. The changes proposed will revolutionize education in America. **These subjects must be taught in homogeneous classrooms with all students on the same instructional levels.** This is the change that will solve the problems created by social promotions.

In the past, the below-grade-level students were placed with average-level and above-average-level students for language arts and basic mathematics, which created an impossible situation for teachers and students. In addition, it resulted in students not having a full period of instruction on their levels. Those who were hurt the most were the ones who needed the full period to bring them up to grade level, which, in far too many cases, never happened. The gaps followed them all throughout their days in school.

The AUG Plan was conceived to correct this main problem caused by social promotion and students not being taught on their instructional levels. With the AUG Plan, there is no retention or need for social promotion. All students are promoted and educated on their instructional levels in language arts and basic mathematics in the elementary school.

There is no need for retention if no students fails in the elementary school. The one major cause of the problems in the elementary school has been caused by social promotion and the way the curriculum is set up. Socially promoted students are sent up to the receiving grades and not given the whole instructional period on their levels in language arts and/or basic mathematics. They may have a third of the period or less being taught on their levels. Their instructional levels are not used to determine where to begin their class work. Receiving teachers are faced with the impossible tasks of adding below-grade-level students to their preparation schedules.

What happens? Instead of having two language arts or basic mathematics preparations a day, teachers have to take instructional time away from the grade-level and above-grade-level students to teach the below-grade-level students. This is an impossible task. All students in the class lose valuable instructional time on the two most important subjects taught in the elementary school. How does one know this is happening? Just look at the results of state and national test score results.

Elementary schools have not corrected the problem they created. Promoting students who are not ready for middle school has been done for years. No one has come up with an organizational plan to correct the problem of students not reading on grade level and not mastering basic mathematics. In 1978, I conceived the plan that would solve the problem. It is a scheduling program called the AUG Plan.   The answer is inexpensive and reasonable. Why pay about $3 million or even $127,000 to have companies correct the problem?[75, 76]

The problems in the elementary school are solved in two steps. First, having all teachers teaching language arts at the same time and all teachers teaching basic mathematics at the same tine. Second, placing all students on their instructional levels in these subjects and receiving the full period of instruction that makes success unavoidable. No one in the classroom is above or below other students in the homogeneous classroom.   The self-concept and self-esteem are going to be positive for all students.

Subjects To Be Taught In The Homogeneous Classrooms

Reading

Reading should be taught in a two-period block early in the instructional day. The teachers would send students from the heterogeneous homerooms to the homogeneous classrooms where their units are being taught on their individual instructional levels. Teachers should have only a few units to prepare for each day instead of many levels and units that are present in the heterogeneous homerooms. Their level/units should be touching. (For example, units 11, 12, 13 or units 3, 4, 5).

There is no need to retain students or to worry about social promotion. Their instructional needs will be being met with this Plan. They all are in classrooms where all students are on the same level. They will have success on their instructional levels because teachers make success unavoidable for all students. Also students who have mastered a skill can assist others who are having trouble.

The homogeneous classrooms are comprised of all average students. No one in the room is below level or above level of the other students. It is a very positive learning environment, allowing students to move successfully at their own pace. Frustration and boredom are removed from the environment. Students feel good about the progress they are making. With students on the same levels, whatever is covered is within their comprehension level. For the teachers, they are not working in an impossible situation. Students go to the teachers who are teaching their units. They may be on-grade-level, below-grade level or up-a-grade-level.

Teaching only touching units in language arts benefits both teachers and students. When three preparations are needed for the class, students have the advantage of hearing the other two units while they are doing seat work. If they have a problem with a skill, there are students in the class that may be able to assist them in learning the skill. Students are able to work at their own rates. They can move up to the next level when they reach 80% mastery on all their skills. The goal is to make students independent readers and on-grade-level by the end of fifth grade so they will be prepared for middle school. The majority of students should be on-grade level by the end of third grade.[77]

One very important task that teachers should do is to take the printable Dolch sight list and have students memorize all the sight words on their grade level. There are 40 pre-primer words, 52 primer words, 41 grade one words, 46 grade two words and 41 grade three words.[78] Mastery of the Dolch list must be 100% in every grade. This will help to hasten student's ability to read successfully.

Basic Mathematics: counting, addition, subtraction, multiplication, division, measurements and fractions

Basic mathematics are taught by all teachers at the same time in homogeneous classrooms for one period block after the language arts class. Students go to the teachers who are teaching their units. They are placed in the class according to their instructional levels. If teachers on their grade levels are not teaching their basic mathematics units they go either up a grade or down a grade to teachers who are teaching their units.

Mathematics teachers may have at most two preparations a day, and the preparations must be similar. Mathematics teachers may not teach low, middle or high skills in the same class period. The students must have similar skills in order for learning differences not to be greater in the class. Students complete units at 100% mastery on the unit tests. The goal is for all students to master all math skills before moving on to the next level. For example, mastering counting before addition; mastering addition before subtraction; mastering subtraction before multiplication; mastering multiplication before division; mastering division before measurements; mastering measurements before fractions, and mastering fractions.

Experience has taught educators that students cannot handle middle school math if they have not mastered basic mathematics. They cannot handle high school math if they have not mastered basic mathematics. Just ask any middle school math teacher which students cannot make it in middle school math and ask any high school math teacher which students cannot handle high school math. There are students in middle school and high school that do not know their basic mathematics. The elementary schools must teach students basic mathematics before they are ready for middle school. The failures of the elementary schools to do this are seen in the low state and national math tests scores in grades eight, twelve and in the exit exams.

A big positive benefit with the AUG Plan is that students do not know where the other students are going unless those students tell them or they are on the same units. There is no negative effect as great as when students are singled out and sent to a class to receive remedial instruction.

This plan has positive effects on students regarding how they feel about themselves and the amount of discipline needed in the school. Teachers have fewer class preparations for these subjects, and they feel good about how well the students are doing because they are teaching in a way that makes success unavoidable.

Movements of Students

Physical Education, Music and Art

For physical education, music and art, students will go by heterogeneous homeroom for these subjects, if their classes are taught by specialists. The school may provide other areas for these subjects to be taught. After the class period is over, the students return to their grade level homeroom.

First Grade

Students in the first grade only move during language arts if they have to be moved up to a grade level that is teaching their instructional levels. After the language arts class is over, they return to their first grade homerooms.

This is also true if first grade students have to move up to a grade for basic mathematics instruction. After the basic mathematics class is over, they return to their grade level homerooms.

Grades Two through Five

Movement of students may vary. For language arts levels and basic mathematics levels, students in these grades go to the teachers who are teaching their level units.

For some students, their units may be taught in their homerooms, which now have become homogeneous classrooms. Other students may have to go to other classrooms to be on their instructional levels. If their level is taught in a lower grade level, they would have to go to the teacher teaching their levels. If their levels were taught in a higher-grade-level classroom, they would have to go up a grade level to the teacher teaching their levels. When the language arts and basic mathematics classes are over, students would return to their heterogeneous homerooms for their other subjects which are taught on grade level.

If two teachers team-teach on their grade level

If two teachers decided one would teach science and the other would teach social studies and health, the teachers would not move. Teachers would teach their subjects to their homeroom. The next period the students would exchange rooms, and the teachers would teach their subjects a second time.

This is an overview of what the AUG Plan is. The following chapters will further explain the Plan and how to implement it in a school.

CHAPTER 11

THE NEED FOR A NEW ORGANIZATIONAL PLAN FOR THE ELEMENTARY SCHOOL

As a result of the search of the literature and overview of the major problems, here is a summary of where we are today regarding elementary education.

There are many problems with the way elementary schools educate students. These problems are the basic causes why middle schools and high schools are not able to have higher tests scores. The problems in education begin in the way elementary schools prepare students for the middle schools, which is carried over to the high schools. Because the causes of school problems begin in the elementary schools, the place to correct them is in the elementary schools.

The problems basically center around only two subjects: language arts (reading, language, spelling and writing) and basic mathematics (counting, addition, subtraction, multiplication, division, measurements and fractions).

With the present plan for advancement, promotion without academic achievement is the norm. Students are being promoted who have not met the academic requirements for placement in the middle school. The result is that receiving teachers are getting students whose academic needs are not being met. Teachers are frustrated because having so many levels to prepare for and teach is impossible. There's not enough time to teach all levels in the alloted time period, and many students go without being taught on their levels and get behind every year. The above-grade level students in a regular classroom suffer boredom. The below-grade level students in a regular classroom suffer frustration. The on-grade level students do fine but **all students lose valuable instructional time which needs to be shared with the below and above grade level students.** The results are receiving teachers are getting students above-grade level (needs not being met), students on-grade level (all needs met), and students not on-grade level (needs not being met), a major problem for teachers. One teacher cannot meet the educational needs of all these students in one classroom.

It is not fair for the grade level students having to give up their instructional time for other level/units students. All of this is related to the teaching of the two foundational subjects in the elementary school: **language arts and basic mathematics.**

The biggest setback is the instructional time each group receives in these two most important elementary school subjects. With a change in the organizational plan of teaching students, the problem can be solved. The success of an educational program is with the teachers who have an educational plan that makes success unavoidable for all students.

In my opinion, the worse thing that has set education back is state testing. This does not improve language arts or basic mathematics. Can anyone show the benefits of state testing? All it does is cost us huge sums of money, takes valuable instructional time away from students and wastes the valuable time of trained teachers who were trained to teach students. I do not know one university that prepares teachers to teach test taking. If teachers were allowed to do what they were trained to do, the quality of education and test scores would show the results. If the schools do next year what they have done these past few years, the situation would continue to get worse each year. The problems will not be corrected.

Unless students have mastered language arts and basic mathematics in the sending grades, they will create the same problems for the teachers in the receiving grades. The problems that resulted in students not being on grade level in the elementary school will increase each year and the test scores will remain the same or will go down if the present educational plan in elementary schools remains the same.

Students who have mastered language arts and basic mathematics each year are ready for the next grade and will be prepared for middle school. Those who are socially promoted will not be ready for their next grade or the middle school when they arrive there. The below-grade level students always end up at the bottom of their classrooms year after year. This has to stop. The elementary schools need a new plan to adequately educate all students.

A new educational plan is necessary to correct the problems caused by social promotion. Under the present situation, no one has come up with a plan that could correct the results of social promotion. I emphatically believe the AUG Plan will solve the problems in education that began in the elementary schools.

CHAPTER 12

UNDERSTANDING THE BELL SHAPE CURVE AND INTELLIGENCE

Each student is special and unique. All students are valuable. All students must be educated to their maximum potential. There is no one educational plan in the elementary schools that will educate all students unless it makes provision for educating students on their instructional levels.

When one thousand people are taken and charted, the distribution is called the Gaussian distribution, which is named after the famous mathematician, Carl Friedrich Gauss.[79] The Gaussian distribution is a pattern for the distribution of a set of values which follows a bell shape curve.[80]

Intelligence and IQ by Dr C. George Boeree[81]

under 70 developmental disability *			2.2%
70-80 borderline intellectual functioning*			6.7%
80-90 low average	"	"	16.1%
90-110 average	"	"	50.0%
110-120 high average	"	"	16.1%
120-130 superior	"	"	6.7%
above 130 very superior	"	"	2.2%

1 s d below/above mean (85-115) contains 68% of all scores

2 s d below/above mean (70-130) contains 95% of all scores

3 s d below/above mean (55-145) contains 99.7% of all scores

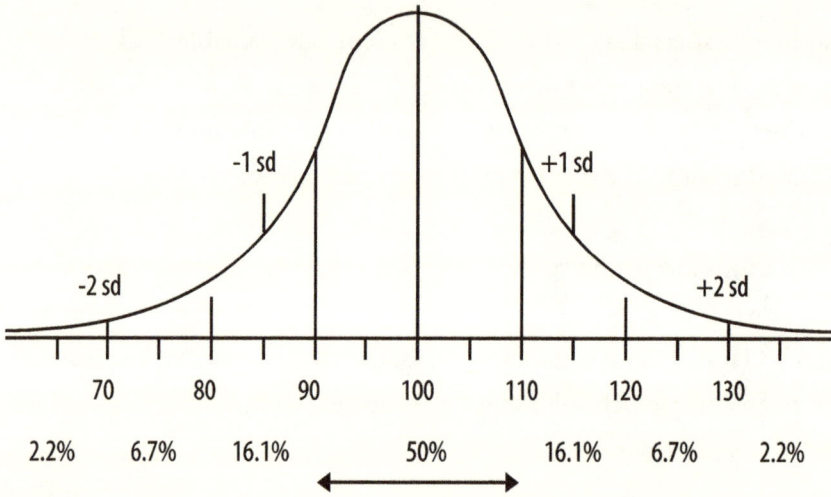

Bell shape curve of normal distribution based on students' IQ[82]

The Bell Shape Curve in Understanding Student's IQ and Meeting Student's Instructional Level Needs

In the homeroom situation, there is the possibility for students to range in IQ's of 70-130 plus in classes. How all students are placed in grade level homerooms according to the AUG Plan allows for the wide range of IQ's in each homeroom.

In former days many students were placed in classes based on their IQ scores. There were the very superior and superior students together in a room. The average and low average students were in another room and the mentally retarded mostly not enrolled. This is not the picture today.

The normal distribution of students means that students with an IQ above 130 are very superior, but the total is just 2.2% of the total population. The next group with an IQ between 120–130 are superior, but the total is just 6.7% of the total population. The next group with an IQ between 110–120 are the high average, but the total is just 16.1% of the total population. The biggest group with an IQ between 90–110 are the average, but the total is 50% of the total population. The next group with an IQ of 80–90 are the low average, but the total is just 16.1% of the total population. Finally, those with an IQ between 70–80 are borderline intellectual functioning which is about 6.7% of the total population.

One can better understand why the homerooms were formed for grade level subjects, and the classrooms were formed having all teachers teaching language arts and basic mathematics at the same time each day in order for students to go to classes where their instruction levels were being taught.

Homerooms

This information will help one to better understand the AUG Plan. In the heterogeneous homerooms the IQ range of students may be 70-130, from the borderline functioning to the superior. The grade level subjects are taught in this setting and small groups are used during the teaching periods. Due to the wide range of IQ's, the students who can read on grade level and know basic mathematics can assist the groups members who may be weak in these subjects as they work together to solve problems.

Classrooms

In the homogeneous classrooms, the students are placed according to their instructional levels/units. Everyone in the classroom is on the same level with the other students. They are all average students in each class of language arts and basic mathematics. No one is above or below them in the subject. Hence there is no frustration or boredom in the classrooms. In these classrooms, there must be 80% or higher mastery of the subject matter before moving on to the next level/units.

These are the classrooms where teachers must make success unavoidable for every student in language arts and basic mathematics. The reason for this is that success for all future education depends on a solid foundation in language arts and basic mathematics. When mastery of these subjects are achieved, students will be prepared to handle all future education.

Pygmalion In The Classroom

A study was conducted involving teacher expectations. There were two grade level classes.[83][84] Students were randomly selected from 18 different classrooms. One teacher was told the students had an IQ about 70, which is borderline intellectual functioning. The second teacher was told the students had an IQ about 120, which is high average.

At the end of the year, the performance of each class was revealed. Class one students improved remarkably to gains of +8.42 and the other class had gains of +3.80 which was performing on the average. What was one factor in the performance of students? The expectation of teachers. When class one was having problems understanding the material, the teacher spent more time getting the lesson over because these were "smart" students with an IQ about 120. For the other class teacher, when the students were having problems understanding the material, the teacher spent less time getting the lesson over because these were not "smart" students with an IQ about 70.

There are at least two conclusions that can be made.

• First, and most importantly, student performance was the result of teacher expectation. Class one teacher made success unavoidable for students thinking their IQ's were about 120. If they did not understand the material, it was the teacher's fault and not the students because they were smart. The teacher spent more time explaining the material.

• Secondly, the teacher thinking the IQ's were about 70, if the students did not understand the material, it was not the teacher's fault. Some students just could not get it. The teacher went on having some students who just would not understand the material. This teacher was not making success unavoidable for all students by not taking more time to explain the lesson until the students understood the concepts.

With the one class, the teacher thought the IQ's were 120, and the students performed on the basis of teacher expectation. The other class teacher thought these were borderline students who were limited in knowledge and some just could not understand. There was no need to take more time to explain for those who still had problems understanding the material. This teacher's expectation was low. Result, performance was based on teacher expectation.

One suggestion for parents: have your children in classes where teachers make success unavoidable for every student in language arts and basic mathematics. You should ask the teachers what their expectations are for your children. If they say that it is up to the students, look for another teacher, one who makes success unavoidable.

I believe it is important for students, parents and educators to understand the complexities of the student populations. If students are going to be properly educated, teachers should be able to educate students beginning at their instructional levels in language arts and basic mathematics until they have mastered these two foundational subjects. The elementary schools should schedule language arts and basic mathematics to be taught at the same time for all grades in order for students to go to the teachers who are teaching their instructional levels/units. These two subjects should be taught first thing in the morning while students are alert. Language arts should be two periods and basic mathematics one period every day.

There are some students who have intellectual and developmental disabilities that can function in the elementary school setting. An organization to contact about this for additional information about intellectual and developmental disabilities is: The Arc, 1825 K Street, NW, Suite 1200, Washington, DC 20006 (800-433-5255).

*The author has taken the liberty to change the original chart labels to the more acceptable terms used today.

CHAPTER 13

THE THEORY FOR THE ORGANIZATION OF HOMEROOMS AND CLASSROOMS

Organization of heterogeneous homerooms

The plan for heterogeneous homeroom composition is based on the concept of treating all students fairly and not putting anyone in a place where his or her self-worth will be diminished. Knowingly or unknowingly, bullying is allowed to continue, many times creating situations that have a negative effect on students.

By having groups in heterogeneous homerooms made up of students below-grade, on-grade and above-grade levels, students who have mastered language arts and basic mathematics can assist their group mates who need help with their other grade level subjects (science, social studies, health, physical education, music and art). Sub-groups formed, within each homeroom, will comprise all levels of students. Within the groups, if there are students who are weak in reading and/or basic mathematics, there are those within each group to help these students. Everything is there to assure that all students can work together productively and successfully. Students are given the opportunity to build up and not tear down fellow students.

Not being able to read on-grade level does not cause a student to feel less self-worth because that skill is not required of all students. All students are in a successful learning environment and can use their skills for the success of their group.

A major factor with every heterogeneous homeroom is that the same outside community makeup is also formed in every homeroom. Students from every socio-economic, racial and cultural backgrounds are placed together in one similar setting for their education. By learning to work productively in the homeroom group, they can take those learned skills back into their homes and communities.

By setting up heterogeneous homerooms, here is the place where major discipline problems can be solved. If there were a problem in the neighborhood, on the school bus, with students that carpool and/or walk to school, that problem may carry over into the homeroom if these students are in the same homeroom. By considering these areas where school problems may begin, one can plan ahead to see that the situations have been adequately addressed before students have been assigned to homerooms by placements according to the AUG Plan.

All heterogeneous homerooms are taught on grade level.

Promoting all students every year keeps them up with their peers and allows them to have grade level subjects taught to them in the heterogeneous homerooms. This solves the problem of having older students in the same class caused by failing grades. They will be promoted each year and taught on their instruction levels in classrooms. Failing students several times in elementary school makes them older and bigger than their classmates and unable to go out for sports in high school while they are still in the middle school.

This also corrects the major problems for teachers who have too many students on different levels in language arts and/or basic mathematics as these subjects are taught in classrooms and not homerooms.

There are no major problems teaching grade level subjects in the elementary school as long as there are students available within each group to help below-grade-level students.

Organization of homogeneous classrooms

Remediation is caused because students have not been properly taught. If teachers would not move ahead with their teaching while leaving students behind who have not mastered the basic skills, there would be fewer students requiring remediation. Every teacher should have the practice of forming subgroups in order to make sure every student masters the basic skills in the subjects taught in classrooms.

One way to accomplish this is to have students that have mastered the skills assist students still having problems who need more time to reach mastery. This does not take more of the teacher's time, but frees the teacher's time by using students who have mastered the skills to assist those who are still working on mastery. This is done in small groups within the classrooms in language arts and basic mathematics.

Homogeneous classroom composition is based on the concept of solving the problems caused by social promotion. Presently students who are below-grade level, on-grade level and above-grade level are placed in the same home-rooms for all subjects.

When teachers promote students who have not mastered language arts and basic mathematics to their next grade levels, these subjects are taught in the re-ceiving grades homogeneous classrooms where the students are taught on their instruction levels. This way, teachers have not failed to do their jobs. Students will be taught on their instructional levels, having no gaps in these subjects in the elementary schools. The teachers will feel fulfilled teaching all students on their instructional levels by making success unavoidable for all students in language arts and basic mathematics.

All homogeneous classrooms are taught on instructional levels

By forming homogeneous classrooms in which language arts and basic mathematics are taught, all subjects are taught on the students' instructional levels. There is no need for retention. Each year in the elementary school, the students will be taught in this setting until they leave the elementary school. By the end of the fifth grade all students should be on grade level. For the above-grade-level students, they will be able to move on to higher levels without being bored in the classrooms in these subjects. This major change will encourage parents to leave their above-average students in the elementary schools knowing they will be challenged to advance in language arts and basic mathematics.

The only way to solve this major problem is to teach these subjects in homogeneous classrooms where all students are taught on their instructional levels and not in heterogeneous homerooms. Placing all three levels in the same classroom is unfair to each student. It results in every teacher having to teach all students who are on different instructional levels in the same room. This wide span of teaching many different units/levels successfully is an impossible task. It requires much more preparation time for the teachers and results in much less instructional time for the students. Further, it is a terrible learning environment for both teachers and students.

For students, it places students who may be bored, average or frustrated in the same setting—an unfair and unjust situation where each group receives less than a fair amount of instructional time on their instructional levels and/or units each day.

For the teachers, it causes frustration, and takes the joy of teaching away. By placing students according to their instructional levels with students on the same levels and units regardless of their grade levels makes success unavoidable in teaching language arts and basic mathematics. Teachers can adequately do a better job teaching; the students will be successful; teacher frustration will be removed, and the joy of teaching will return for all because they all can experience success and fulfillment in what they are doing.

Because classes are homogeneous, every student is an average student in the class, and there is no frustration or boredom. It is an ideal situation for both students and teachers. Each feels good about what is happening and looks forward to returning and being successful in learning and/or teaching. Students return to their homerooms, have experienced success and have good feelings about improving their language arts and basic mathematics skills.

No one knows where students go for classroom subjects unless they were in the same classroom. Each student experiences success in the classroom; hence, no student is ridiculed or put down by other students.

Another great benefit is when students who are below-grade level find themselves in classrooms where all students are on the same instructional levels. In fact, all students are on the same levels in each classroom. That is not the case in the homeroom. With the small group organization within the homeroom, each group has all the knowledge available to them to get the job done. Learning is a team effort in which everyone has an opportunity to make a contribution.

The AUG approach is the answer to using social promotion and homogeneous classrooms as a balanced, fair method of educating below-grade, on-grade, and above-grade level students in language arts and basic mathematics. The needs of each group are fully met with no one being held back and all moving at their own rates without discrimination.

In the present set up in the elementary schools, the only ones having their needs fully met are the on-grade level students. The below-grade students are not struggling to get on grade level. The above-grade levels students who are held back are frustrated by material they already know. In the AUG Plan, everyone's needs are fully met in the most important fundamental subjects that are taught in the elementary schools.

Consider the story of a third grade boy who benefited from the AUG plan. He was in third grade when the AUG Plan was put into effect and was reading on first grade level. He had to go down to second grade for language arts because first grade reading level was not being taught in third grade. Because all students were moving at the same time to go for language arts, so no one knew where he was going. He noticed that students who were younger than he were reading better than he. He worked harder to advance his level/units. By March, in fifth grade, (two and a half years later) he was reading on grade level. Instead of being a student who was not on grade level, he was promoted to fifth grade reading on grade level. He graduated from high school. Fifteen years later, he was seen by me with a paperback book in his back pocket. He now loves to read.

THE DIRECTIONS FOR SETTING UP THE AUG PLAN

How does one set up the homerooms?

Lists containing necessary information must be completed at the end of the school year for each homeroom. The office secretary will give each teacher Form 1A showing the present students and their addresses. The teacher will fill in the requested information under each heading. Form 1A will have space on the back of the sheet to share comments that will assist in placing students for the next year. These types of information that are needed are bits such as: what students should be separated, what two students can be placed together, what students have medical problems and other factors that will help in forming the new homerooms.

If a school is beginning the AUG Plan before the school year is over, the homeroom teachers can give a list of students on Form 1A listing the requested data.

Most schools will have teachers filling out the student enrollment giving information on name, sex, race, reading level/unit and basic mathematics level and unit.

The teacher may also have information on how the student arrives at school and if student has special needs. In some cases the secretary may have this information on the computer and can print out that information.

It is best to have this information at the beginning of the school year, but the AUG Plan can be set in motion at any time; it is never too late.

Use at the end of the school year for listing present homeroom membership. Return to Office Secretary.

Teacher Name_____

Circle Grade level: Pre-K K 1 2 3 4 5 6   Circle Homeroom: A B C D E F

Full Name and Address of Student	Sex (M/F)	Race	Arrival (bus, car, walk...)	Reading Level or unit	Math Level or unit	Comments

Chart 1 Sample of Form 1A

Use at the beginning of the new school year for listing receiving teachers' homerooms.

Teacher_____

Circle Grade: Pre-K K 1 2 3 4 5 6   Circle Homeroom: A B C D E

Full Name and Address of Student	Sex (M/F)	Race	Arrival (bus, car, walk...)	Reading Level or unit	Math Level or unit	Comments

Chart 1 Sample of Form 2B

After all of the lists are available from the teachers Form 1A, the school secretary needs to supply a list of all incoming students with the same information listed. A professional staff member who is responsible for placing new students can supply the information for Form 1A. All this information is given to the professional who is going to form new homerooms for the coming year using Form 2B.

How many homerooms will a school have?

If one uses twenty-five students per homeroom, the following charts will help one in knowing that answer. Some schools may choose to have less than twenty-five students per homeroom and some may choose to have up to thirty in a homeroom. Form 1A has lines for up to thirty students per homeroom.

Chart 2 to find out number of homerooms needed per grade

School size,	Number of students in each grade,							Rooms needed
	K	1	2	3	4	5	6	
375	25-1	50-2	75-3	100-4	125-5	150-6	175-7	15 required

Chart 3 to find out numbers of homerooms needed per grade level

25-1	150- 6	275-11	400-16	525-21	650-26	775-31
50-2	175- 7	300-12	425-17	550-22	675-27	800-32
75-3	200- 8	325-13	450-18	575-23	700-28	825-33
100-4	225- 9	350-14	475-19	600-24	725-29	850-34
125-5	250-10	375-15	500-20	625-25	750-30	875-35

How would the person making up the homerooms begin?

For an example, let's use a student body of 375 students requiring 15 homerooms. There will be 1 homeroom for kindergarten, 2 for first, 3 for second, 4 for third, 3 for fourth and 2 for five. Nothing needs to be done for kindergarten because there will be only one homeroom. The only check is for first names.

What column does one begin with first?

The goal is to end the task with the same number of student characteristics in each homeroom (sex, race, disabled, top, middle and low students in reading and basic mathematics).

It is suggested to begin with the reading column first and then the name column followed by math, sex, race, how they arrive at school disability and lastly, the address column. Each homeroom is to be as heterogeneous and as similar as possible. All of the homerooms have the same composition. Every homeroom is an identical representation of the community in composition.

There are many other ways to do the job. Using a computer to set up the homerooms according to these factors is the best timesaving way to do it. But if a computer is not available and/or no one knows how to program it, then the next best method may be the old fashioned way of doing it by hand.

The by-hand approach does work

Here is how it is done. In the example, third grade is the choice. If it is done by hand, **be sure to use pencil and eraser because one will need to change names as changes are made in order to keep balance in the homerooms.**

The person making the list has 4 completed homeroom Forms 1A from school year 2010-11. Information taken from Forms 1A are placed on Forms 2B to make the 4 new homerooms, filling line and columns for each entry. Then one takes the first factor, such as reading skill levels and units and begins to fill each homeroom placing top, average and finally low in each homeroom. The same is done with the top, average and low mathematics levels and units. This is done to balance the rooms academically.

Next place students according to sex, the same number of girls in each room and also boys. There may be odd numbers and some classes may be one short. As new grade level students arrive they are placed where the next girl or boy should be placed. The other factors of reading and mathematics are not used after the school year starts. Next do the multiracial column. Same sex is not important in racial placement. Place at least two racial of the same race in the homerooms. This all depends on how many racial students are on grade level. The majority may be black, white or another. Remember no single girl, boy or student of color should ever be placed in isolation. This may never happen, but if it does, and there is only one girl, boy or student of color in a grade level, do what is in the best placement for the student.

The next column is disability. Many times there may be no students in this category. Sometimes there may be only one in a school or one on grade levels. The IEP's must state that the student can be mainstreamed or if the student can attend pre-arranged classes.

Now comes the most difficult task—checking to see that the academic balance remains in-tact for each homeroom. There may be two or more students with the same first name. To correct this, exchange students who have the same characteristics in the sex, race, reading, math columns.

When list changes have to be made in homeroom placement, one should change those names that have all the columns the same. After the lists are made, the administrator should look over the lists to see if further changes need to be made.

One must check with the secretary to receive the information on students who were not in the school from the previous year in order to receive their school placement facts to include them in the placement for the coming year.

After the school year begins, the only factors that should be followed are name, sex and multiracial in placing new students in homerooms. Students that are transferred within the school district come with their school records with them. Students who come into the school after the year begins may not have their school records with them. Placement tests must be given to determine their reading levels and units and mathematics levels and units for these new students.

Another method to form homerooms

Take the first Form 1A and place all the students for that grade level on to the new Form 2B's. Then take the second Form 1A and do the same. Do this for all of the 1A Forms. Also get the information from the office of all incoming students for the coming year. One has to be very careful in doing this to make sure that balance is maintained for each homeroom and in every column.

REMEMBER after placements are completed and school has started, new students are added to homerooms based only on numbers of students relating to name, sex and race. No students are moved from homeroom to homeroom after school has started in order to keep the balance of the homerooms.

SECTION FOUR
THE IMPLEMENTATION
OF THE AUG PLAN
(CHAPTERS 15–20)

CHAPTER 15

HOW TO USE HOMOGENEOUS CLASSROOMS AND HETEROGENEOUS HOMEROOMS TO ADEQUATELY TEACH ALL STUDENTS

All students are not identical. Their intelligence spans a band from 70 IQ to 130 IQ: This includes borderline functioning, low average, average, high average and superior students. Many grades may have this range in the student body. Some of the learners are slow, some average, and others fast. The main difference between students is time on task. In other words, how long does it take to master a skill? How can one adequately plan to meet the educational needs of all students?

The average IQ, 80–120, low to high, is 82% of the population. The high is 120–130 and the borderline is 70–80. Educators in the past have formed three levels of classes on grade level. There were classes for the below-average students, the average students, and the above-average students. The below average include many minority students and students who did not have English as their main language. It also includes the students with lower IQs.

Today with social promotion as a common practice, students are promoted based on age and not academic achievement. This means receiving teachers are receiving students who are not prepared for grade level work. As these students continue to be advanced each year, their learning gaps widen.

Every receiving teacher has an impossible task to teach students who are on too many different levels in language arts and basic mathematics in elementary grades. There is no way to correct this with only one teacher in the room to teach all of the students on their instructional levels. Many teachers are facing this situation year after year.

A Better Plan

There are problems with social promotion. Students should not be held back in the elementary schools. The problems are corrected when all students each day are taught language arts during the same time and basic mathematics during the same time in homogeneous classrooms.

The AUG Plan calls for language arts to be taught at the same time for all grades in the elementary school. It also calls for basic mathematics to be taught at the same time for all grades. Both are taught in homogeneous classrooms early in the instructional day. The students are taught on their instructional levels in both subjects. Some students may have to go down a grade or up a grade for this to happen if their instructional levels are not being taught on their grade level.

Because many students may have to leave their homerooms to be in classrooms that are teaching their instructional levels in different rooms, no one knows where these students are going unless they are in the same classroom. This helps to build a good self concept. The students are reading on their levels and moving at their own rate of learning. They are having success in their school work. In the past, students were pulled out of classrooms for remediation. These were mainly students who were not on grade level. They were singled out by reason of leaving the classroom for instruction. With the AUG Plan, many students move to go to teachers that are teaching their units/levels. Because so many students are moving, other students know they are going to language arts or basic mathematics. They do not know to which grade levels the other students are going. There is no stigma when students move in the AUG Plan. The self-concepts are positive for all students.

In these subjects, students are with other students who are on the same levels/units. Everyone in the class is an average student. The purpose is to make the instructional level as similar as possible to give the students a better learning environment which will help make success unavoidable.

The classrooms are integrated because the homerooms are integrated. The classrooms are homogeneous because the subject matter is within the instructional level of all students.

When the language arts period is over, the students go to their mathematics classrooms. When the mathematics period is over, the students return to their heterogeneous homerooms for the subjects that are taught on grade level. The advantage of this plan is that no students are put down because of where they go for language arts and for mathematics. Only students who are in their classroom know the level of other students. The differences are so small that they view themselves as average students

Teachers have all students who are on similar units with this plan. It is easier each day for teachers to prepare for classes. They can teach well in an environment made to order for them. There is no teacher to blame because of the impossible differences that created a depressing instructional program. All students benefit from the instruction during the whole class. Students who are having trouble with a concept can be assisted by those who have mastered it. Teachers teach in a way that makes success unavoidable. Students are able to complete their levels and then move up to their next levels.

In basic mathematics, students go to the teachers who are teaching their units. They stay in that classroom until they complete the units being taught. When they complete those units, they move up to the teachers who are teaching their next levels. The students move at their own rate of completion.

Teachers prepare for the reading and mathematics levels they are teaching. When the periods for reading and mathematics are over, students leave their homogeneous classrooms and go to their heterogeneous homerooms to be taught grade level subjects that are on grade level.

By teaching students on their instructional levels in language arts and mathematics in the elementary classrooms, social promotion presents no problems having students in grade level homerooms learning their other subjects. While many different levels of language arts and mathematics are present in the homerooms, no gaps are allowed to go unaddressed. The classrooms are there to meet students on their instructional levels. There is no need to hold students back and place them in situations which are beyond their control and treat them in an belittling way. There is a way to educate them in an honorable and fair way with no discrimination. Schools are where students are to be educated and not held back or singled out for ridicule or scorn.

These problems which caused students being below grade level have existed far too long. Students have dropped out of school, have been forced to get into unacceptable habits and troubles, and no one has come up with the solution. Here it is. The problem is created by the way that many elementary schools are not teaching all students grade level subjects and passing them up to the middle school unprepared to do middle school academic work. The middle school and high school problems have been passed up by the elementary schools, which have not prepared students for grade level work. Students are not being taught to read and to learn basic mathematics in the elementary schools. South Carolina State School Superintendent, Mick Zais said, "If students do not learn how to read in elementary school, they face enormous challenges and barriers. We must emphasize reading because it is the most important subject students need to master to be successful in school."[85]

"If students do not master each math in basic mathematics before they move on to the next math, they will not be able to understand or handle middle and high school math courses," said Daniel Y. Tittiris.[86] Language arts and mathematics are basics that must be mastered in elementary school for students to be successful in all future education.

CHAPTER 16

HOW TO TEACH BASIC MATHEMATICS IN THE ELEMENTARY SCHOOL

By Daniel Y. Tittiris, B.S., M.Ed. Teacher of the Year, 2012

It has always been my desire to be the best mathematics teacher students could possibly ever have. During the course of my tenure as a mathematics teacher in a public high school, I have noticed a severe lack of basic mathematics skills in students. This lack of adequate preparation has a debilitating effect on the readiness level of students for the abstract reasoning skills necessary for higher-level mathematics. Some high school students have never mastered the basic skills of addition, subtraction, multiplication, division, measurements and fractions; and this lack of mastery translates into poor mathematical achievement. There is a sense of urgency within the educational community to reverse the trend of poor mathematical readiness that is being instilled.

Counting

One of the most basic mathematical skills is the ability to count. From a young age many children learn how to count because of the influence and instruction of their parents. Counting is a necessary component of human existence, for without a coherent counting system it would be difficult to communicate with one another. Learning to count is an important part of child development because counting helps children make a sense of their immediate surroundings and communicate their needs and wants. For example, if Tom wants his mother to give him one more cookie he must learn how to express his desire for one additional cookie. He could grunt or point at the cookie but counting and expressing his desire as a number is a much more efficient way of communication. If children never learn to count, they will not be able to make progress in their communication skills and this will have an adverse effect on their development.

I remember that one of my proudest accomplishments as a kindergarten student was counting from 1 to 100. This accomplishment may seem trivial to an adult; but, to a 5 year old counting from 1 to 100 provides a sense of completeness and independence. Children who do not master counting should not progress to the next level of mathematical reasoning until they have received appropriate remediation and instruction to insure that counting has been mastered. Many children learn how to count from parents, but it is important for teachers to understand that some children do not have access to an educationally stimulating home environment, and learning how to count may not be a high priority for some parents. This is probably one of the biggest problems in modern education, because without the support of parents at home, students will experience difficulty in school. A parent who does not care about education communicates distain for education to the child, which in turn influences children to develop a negative perspective towards learning and education. I was blessed to have parents, who valued education, and they celebrated educational successes, such as the first time I was able to count from 1 to 100.

Counting is the foundation of number sense, and the ability to count is an important skill that children will use at any level of their educational careers. Without mastery of counting, children cannot effectively communicate with others and, as a result, frustration and a sense of worthlessness may set in. I believe that parents must take an active role in teaching their children how to count. However, for children who have parents who do not teach children how to count, the teacher must intervene and provide children with the instruction and attention necessary for every student to master the skill of counting. If children never learn how to count, how can teachers expect that they will succeed at the next levels? Children should not move on to the next level of mathematics until they have mastered counting.

Addition

Not only is it important for children to learn to count, children must also learn how to add numbers and understand how the operation of addition affects the total number of objects present in a given situation. Once a child learns how to count physical objects, he or she should be given deliberate and specific instructions in how to add up these physical objects. This concept can be easily demonstrated by giving children a few objects at a time and then adding additional objects and asking children to provide the teacher with the total amount. For example if you gave Tom two cookies and then asked him to count how many cookies he had you would be reinforcing the concepts of counting. Then if you gave Tom one more cookie and asked him to count how many cookies he had now you would be providing Tom with specific instruction in how one additional object increases the total amount of objects present.

Addition is a relatively simple skill for children to learn because it naturally builds on the concepts of counting. As a child learns how to count from 1 to 10, he or she is also learning how to add 1 to each previous number. Learning how to add successfully is a critical skill for children to master, and it is truly discouraging for high school mathematics teachers to see their students struggling with simple addition rules. I believe that elementary school teachers should not view teaching addition as a trivial topic that does not warrant the full attention and apportionment of instructional resources. Every student should develop a mastery of single digit addition at an early age and then use this knowledge and understanding to progress to multiple digit addition. However, despite the risk of my being redundant, a child should not progress from single digit addition to multiple digit addition without developing mastery of single digit addition. This practice of moving students from one level to the next can have the effect of setting a child up for failure.

If a child is having difficulty adding single digit numbers, then the teacher should exhaust all possible instructional strategies or teaching techniques from the teacher's professional repertoire. The key is for the teacher to never surrender or give up because, in many cases, students can sense whether or not a teacher genuinely believes that the student can succeed. A lack of persuasive encouragement can lead to a child's failure. Teachers should employ the use of objects that are relevant to a student's interest and real life experience to teach abstract concepts of addition to students who struggle with abstract mathematical notation. A teacher could use physical objects to demonstrate to a student that 15 chocolate chips added to 17 chocolate chips is 32 chocolate chips by having the student count and enjoy the chips. The aforementioned technique is superior to simply giving a student an abstract rule of adding 7 to 5 and getting 12 and then carrying the 1 over to the second column and adding it to the 1 of 15 and the 1 of 17 to give 3 in the tens column. This author expects that the reader had to go back and re-read the last sentence due the confusing nature and presentation of the addition rule. This confusing explanation was deliberately included to allow the reader to experience the same level of confusion and frustration that a child may experience with having mathematical rules explained in an abstract manner.

Students need to have mathematical rules explained in a manner that makes mathematical operations make sense and provide students with a sense of relativity to their everyday lives. If students understand the importance of addition and the purpose the operation of addition plays in their lives, they may be more prone to develop mastery of this skill because of the necessity associated with the ability to add numbers. Therefore teachers should require students to develop and demonstrate a mastery of addition rules and facts, especially before they move on the next level of mathematics, which can be one of the most challenging at a lower elementary level: subtraction.

Subtraction

Subtraction is a mathematical skill that follows as a logical extension of addition. Subtraction is the inverse operation of addition, and this can cause problems for students who have struggled to understand concepts related to double digit addition. Subtraction requires students to understand the mathematical manipulation associated with renaming in order to solve problems such as 23 - 17. Students have to understand that correct mathematical manipulation is essential to success in subtraction and future mathematical studies. However, many students struggle with subtraction because of the use of renaming.

Teachers should attempt to use methods which will reinforce the concept of renaming with physical objects. For example, if Tom is having problems understanding that 23 - 17 is equal to 6, then the teacher could give him 23 chocolate chips and then have Tom eat six of the chips and then count how many he had left. The concept of borrowing 1 from 2 in the tens units of 23 to convert 3 to 13 is a difficult abstract concept for some students to understand. However, renaming is a critical skill for elementary school mathematics. Once students recognize the algorithm involved in renaming, additional practice with a wide variety of problems can lead to increased confidence and success.

The teachers have a responsibility to help students overcome struggles with mathematical reasoning, and parents should provide teachers with support at home in order to reinforce what is taught at school. Teachers should provide parents with real-life applications of subtraction which can apply to a student's every day interactions in society. For example, making change from coins is an excellent way of teaching students the importance of subtraction. If students cannot perform simple subtraction operations they may not know how much change they should receive from another individual. Given the role that money and the economy plays in modern society, students have much to gain from a correct understanding of subtraction within the context of purchasing goods and service.

Obviously addition is an easier operation than subtraction, and some students may resent the fact that they are being forced to learn an additional mathematical operation which is more complex. However, parents and teachers should communicate the importance of subtraction as a critical skill for productive members of a modern society. Students need to understand that the skills learned in elementary school will not only transcend the rest of their years in elementary, middle and secondary education but also affect their lives as adults. Failure to develop an adequate understanding of subtraction can have far-reaching negative ramifications for students, and it is the responsibility of teachers and parents to work together to ensure that every student can achieve success and confidence in subtraction. Once students have mastered subtraction of both single and multiple digit numbers with a wide variety of problem contexts they will be ready to progress to learning and applying the skill of multiplication.

Multiplication

Multiplication is one of the most important mathematical skills students must master in elementary school in order to be successful in higher level mathematics. Multiplication takes the concepts learned from addition and introduces the concepts of grouping and increasing amounts of given objects by a set rate. Therefore multiplication is a more complex skill for children to master and many children have to develop a mastery of multiplication skills for the numbers 1 through 12. There can be no exceptions and no teacher should resort to giving students a calculator for these basic multiplication skills. As difficult as it may be for children to learn their multiplication tables, it is a critical skill and many hours must be devoted to the methodical memorization of basic multiplication facts.

The learning associated with multiplication has so many far reaching ramifications that it is negligent for educators to allow students who do not master these skills to advance to the next level. However, the blame must not solely be placed upon educators because parents also bear the burden of responsibility for ensuring that their children are spending adequate time memorizing the basic multiplication facts. Teachers and parents must work together to form partnerships between school home to ensure that children are able to master these critical multiplication skills. If a child struggles with learning basic multiplication facts, then it is the responsibility of teachers to use different learning and teaching strategies to reach a child who may not learn multiplication facts in a conventional manner.

Some students may have difficulty interpreting a multiplication table and may be better suited to having multiplication explained using groups of objects to demonstrate basic multiplication facts. For example, if Tom is struggling with learning his multiplication facts, his teacher or parents could utilize the use of a specific number of pieces of candy to provide instruction and motivation for Tom to learn his multiplication facts. Tom could be shown that 3 groups of 5 candy pieces could be counted out one at a time which would reinforce his counting skills. After developing confidence with counting, Tom could be instructed to add 5 and 5 and 5 together to give him the total number of pieces of candy. After feeling confident with the addition skills, Tom may be able to see 3 groups of 5 can be expressed as 3 x 5 which equals 15. This use of real objects to solidify the concepts of multiplication could be the turning point in many children's struggles with multiplication. The use of incentives to reinforce learning by allowing Tom to eat the candy after he demonstrates a correct understanding of basic multiplication may also help the instructional process.

No matter which method of teaching multiplication facts is employed, students must be held accountable for learning these facts. I believe that social promotion is a great disservice to students who have not mastered their multiplication skills. Students who do not master multiplication skills will experience difficulties with the next level of mathematics and all subsequent mathematical instruction. An understanding of multiplication is essential to success in mathematics and it is my hope that parents and educators will employ all necessary steps, teaching techniques and motivational opportunities to provide every child with the opportunity to succeed in learning his or her multiplication facts. Multiplication is truly one of the most foundational skills that a child must develop in his or her repertoire of mathematical skills, and parents and educators must provide the necessary support and encouragement for every child to experience success.

Division

The next important skill that students need to master after multiplication is division. However, for children to have any chance of understanding and mastering division, they must have a competent mastery of multiplication. Without an understanding of multiplication students will not understand division, which is the inverse operation of multiplication. Division requires children to invert the process of multiplication and this requires the automatic process of reverse multiplication. For example, children should know that 5 x 4 = 20. Therefore, children should understand that 20\ 4 = 5 or 20\5 = 4.

This is why a competent understanding of multiplication rules is absolutely necessary for success in division. Students must know their multiplication tables and be able to recall these important facts immediately. Multiplication skills are critical for success in mathematics and parents and teachers must ensure that each child is held accountable to learn these important facts.

However, division is not simply the reverse of multiplication rules. Students are also required to know how to perform long division, which involves reverse multiplication and subtraction. Long division can be a very arduous process which can cause much frustration to students. I remember this difficult experience with long division in third grade. I did not understand the process of finding the remainder of the long division process and remember staying in during recess to rework every problem I got wrong. The process of long division led to a level of frustration that the author would not want any other child to experience.

Long division also requires students to utilize subtraction to progress through the division process and find the appropriate remainder. Since long division has many steps and utilizes subtraction, students must have mastered these key skills. Therefore, teachers must utilize any teaching technique possible to ensure that students fully understand subtraction rules. Once again, the process of division demonstrates that students should not be allowed to progress to the next level until they have mastered basic mathematics skills.

For students who struggle with division, teachers could consider the use of physical objects to reinforce key division's concepts. Students could be shown how objects can be separated into groups to lead to division. For example, if Tom is shown 30 cookies and asked how many groups he could separate the cookies into, the teacher could help Tom see that 30 cookies could be split into 2 groups of 15, 3 groups of 10, 5 groups of 6 and 6 groups of 5. This could lead a struggling student to a concrete understanding of division. If students can be given the tools to succeed, then a difficult concept such as division can be broken down into individual steps leading students to understanding of an important concept. If students can experience success in mathematics, then they can develop competence and confidence in their abilities.

Measurement and Fractions

• Students also need to understand how to use different instruments to measure amounts of any given object. They should be competent with rounding measurements to the nearest unit of measurement that makes sense for a particular problem. For example, children should know how to measure length of different objects to the nearest inch or centimeter. This can have significant applications to scientific experiments and the use of measurements within the scientific method. Mathematics and science tend to work together forming a symbiotic relationship where mathematics reinforces science and science tends to complement mathematics.

• Students also need to learn how to manipulate fractions. This skill can be one of the most difficult topics for children to master, but it is critical for every child to learn how to add, subtract, multiply and divide fractions.

• Students need to learn how to add and subtract fractions using common denominators, and how to multiply fractions by performing multiplication across the numerators and denominators of fractures.

• Students will also need to learn that the division of fractions requires the use of multiplication of the reciprocal. Teachers may find that using real objects to teach fractions will help reinforce these key concepts with students who typically struggle with fractions. For example, students usually respond positively to fraction problems which include cutting up a pie or cake to eat. This makes the learning process more exciting and allows fractions to be used in a real problem solving situation.

Once again mastery of the basic mathematical operations of addition, subtraction, multiplication and division will provide students with the tools necessary to succeed in manipulating fractions or any other area of upper elementary mathematics. However, students who do not master these important topics will probably struggle in their future mathematical endeavors. Therefore, it is necessary for parents and teachers to work together to ensure the success of students in elementary level mathematics as this foundation may have long lasting effects on a student's chance for academic success in the future.

ADDENDUM - AUG Basic Mathematics Grid and Basic Mathematics

Including the seven maths that make up basic mathematics

1	11	21	31	41	51	61	71	(81)	91
2	12	22	32	42	52	62	(72)	82	92
3	13	23	33	43	53	(63)	73	83	93
+4	14	24	34=	44	(54)	64	74	84	94
5	15	25	35	(45)	55	65	75	85	95
=6	16	26	(36)	46	56	66	76	86	96
7	17	(27)	37	47	57	67	77	87	97
8	(18)	28	38-4	48	58	68	78	88	89
(9)	19	29	39	49	59	69	79	89	99
10	20	30	40	50	60	70	80	90	100

Example: 2+4=6   38-4=34

No calculators allowed in elementary schools: in order for students to learn Basic Mathematics. Calculators are allowed in the middle school and High School.

Ten Basic Mathematics' Maths

1 Counting: 1 to 100

2 Addition: 4+   +4   +4
  counting by 4 = 4 8 <u>12</u> 16 20 24 28 <u>32</u> 36 40 44 48 <u>52</u> 56 60 64 68
3 Subtraction: -4 =   -4   -4   -4

4 Multiplication: 4   3 4 5 6 7 8 9 10   12 13 14 15 16 17
  counting by 4=4 8 12 16 20 24 28 32 36 40 44 48 52 56 60 64 68
5 Division: 4/4   1 2 3   4 5 6 7 8 9 10   12   14   16

Division 2 x 3 = 6 6 / 3 = 2   Do the multiplication (x) and
         3 x 2 = 6 6 / 2 = 3   division (/) for numbers 4–5,
                                   6-7 and 8-9.

6 Fractions: ½ of 50 = 25 (25 50), 1/3 of 99 = 33 (33, 66, 99)
           ¼ of 100 = 25 (25, 50, 75, 100)
           1/5 of 100 = 20 (20, 40, 60, 80, 100)

7 Measurements: Count the last row of multiples of 10 for applications
           to the metric system, for example: 100 mm = 10 cm (count 10),
           70 mm = 7 cm (count 7).

8 Time: 60 seconds = 1 minute, 60 minutes = 1 hour
         24 hours = 1 day, 7 days = 1 week

9 Length: 12 inches = 1 foot, 3 feet = 1 yard.

10 Liquid: 4 gills = 1 pint, 2 pints = 1 quart,
           4 quarts = 1 gallon

All students in Language Arts and Basic Mathematics classes on their insctruction levels. All students are average students in these classrooms.

No failure in elementary schools.

CHAPTER 17

HOW TO TEACH READING IN THE ELEMENTARY SCHOOL

By Jennifer Midgett Meyers, B.S. Elementary teacher

The first thing that I do in the beginning of a school year is to look at the students' standardized test scores from the previous year. I look at these to assess areas of strength and weakness for the child in the previous grade level. I also interview the previous year's teacher to find any information regarding strengths, weaknesses, and reading levels. Once I do those two things, I loosely group the students based on the information that I have and begin my own series of diagnostic testing so that I can make academic decisions based on current findings. The groupings are flexible and as I find additional information such as gains or losses in reading skills, I adjust these groupings. Groupings in my reading class are not permanent. These groups must remain flexible and fluid so that the children are always in the group that best suits their ability level and understanding of the material.

Once these first groupings are completed, I spend time conducting my own series of diagnostics based on the reading curriculum diagnostic tests, accelerated reader reading levels, individualized reading inventories (IRIs), and any online testing that may be available to me through the school system. In using IRIs, I look at reading fluency when the student is reading, as well as vocabulary and comprehension of the material through the student's answers based on a series of questions. I also use the Dolch Word List to determine what level of sight words the student has mastered.[87]

Based on these series of tests, I am able to group the students based on the level of knowledge and skills that they have acquired in reading. These groups are now more "formal," in that the students remain with this group of students until they reach certain milestones, which allow them to progress to other groups. It is not uncommon for a typical classroom to have a wide range of reading abilities. Since this is usually the case, the teacher cannot teach a whole classroom of students with one lesson. If this practice occurs, the gifted students are not challenged, the below grade level students become frustrated, and gaps in learning result. Typically, the only students who benefit in this type of classroom are the narrow group of students who are at grade level and are ready for the material taught. Because of this reality, I advocate teaching reading at one specific time during the day (preferably first thing in the morning) and that a team of teachers teach different reading levels: the AUG Plan. The students go to the classroom that is teaching at their unique level.

The teachers then test the students at regular intervals to chart progress. If teachers notice that a student is progressing quickly and is not challenged by the material, the child is assessed and placed ahead in the appropriate level. If a student finds difficulty in learning the new material, the child can be assessed and moved back to the level where he or she can learn the new information comfortably, without frustration and stress. Once the child experiences success and has a little time practicing the skill that is difficult, it is not uncommon for the child to be moved up to the more advanced level.

The key to this plan working is to have a group of teachers who work well as a team, communicate all of their concerns, challenges, and goals for students with fellow teachers, and the ability to be flexible. In my experience, this practice works best when all teachers have consistent grading, behavior, and homework expectations since the students may be rotating in and out of various classrooms based on skill level.

This plan does require a lot of planning, teamwork, and communication to be successful, but it is in the best interest of the student in eliminating learning gaps that are detrimental to future learning as the student progresses.

In my classroom, I focused on oral reading, comprehension, vocabulary, and skills such as sequencing, story elements, and the required standards presented by the state department of education. When possible, I would make charts and graphic organizers so that the students were constantly working on the story elements, vocabulary, and any new skills that were needed. I truly believe repetition is key in the mastery of reading skills.

The key to any reading instruction is assessment of learning gaps, addressing those gaps before any new learning is added, and seeking to see if new gaps pop up as new material is added. If a student does not master a skill, the student does not move ahead, as reading skills build upon one another. If one skill is missing, the next skill should not be taught until the previous skill is learned. This lays a firm foundation for the child and insures that the student can be successful in the reading classroom.

It is also very important to work on sight words. The Dolch Sight Word List must be memorized by all. The list is available online or at any school supply business.[87] The listing of 220 words are for preschool through grade three.

Traditionally, schools have concentrated on whole classroom instruction, rather than the individual needs of the student. When one concept is taught to the class, then the teacher moves on to teach the next concept. This practice has created a generation of children who are not reading on grade level and have difficulty with comprehension and vocabulary. The individual needs of the students must be met in order for every student to be successful in reading. All students must be successful readers because, all other subjects and disciplines depend upon reading in order to be academically successful.

CHAPTER 18

HOW TO TEACH MIDDLE SCHOOL AND HIGH SCHOOL STUDENTS WHO ARE BELOW GRADE LEVEL IN LANGUAGE ARTS AND/OR BASIC MATHEMATICS

Using the AUG Plan in middle and high schools to teach language arts and basic mathematics in homogeneous classes is recommended when students are performing below grade level. These students may have been promoted to middle or high schools without mastering these elementary grade level subjects. They need to be instructed at their instructional levels in language arts and/or basic mathematics in order to pass the middle and high schools subjects.

When the AUG Plan is followed in the elementary schools, it will improve the quality of students that will be coming into the middle schools. However, the middle and high schools will have to identify those students who need these subjects in order to be able to do the work that is required of them. These classes are to be taught in a way to make success unavoidable. Not mastering language arts and basic mathematics by the time these students enter the upper grades will hamper them from doing acceptable work. Mastering basic reading and mathematics is foundational for one to be successful in all future education.

Once these subjects are mastered, students have a solid foundation and are well prepared to be successful in all future studies. It is when schools fail students in teaching these three subjects that students are not prepared to give back to the community skills that will make this world a better world in which to live.

Reading

The middle and high schools will need to give placement tests to find out which students are below-grade level in language arts. When their reading levels are identified, they need to be taught the skills that will lead them to become independent readers.

The students should be placed in homogeneous reading classes with other students who are on the same units. Students can be drawn from all grades for the middle school class and the high school class. The teacher has only one reading preparations for each class of below-grade level readers. All students in the class should be on similar touching units, making it an average class with no one above or below their levels.

The teacher can make success for all students unavoidable in this setting and have students who can help one another master the skills. The printable Dolch Sight Word List[88] will help those who are having problems with the 220 sight words.

A reading teacher can teach other sections of touching units to other students in the middle and high schools who are on grade units. By making the differences in the homogeneous classroom small, the students will have the benefit of the whole period of instruction. The goal of helping students become independent readers prepares them to be successful in all future learning.

Basic Mathematics—Counting, Addition, Subtraction, Multiplication, Division, Measurements and Fractions

In the middle and high schools, some students are not ready for middle or high school math because they have not mastered basic mathematics in the elementary school. Until basic mathematics are mastered, students are not able to satisfactorily handle any middle or high schools math. These students need to master basic mathematics in which they are weak before starting middle and high school math. Every basic mathematics builds on the former math. If any basic math is not mastered, the students will have major difficulty with all future math.

The math teacher has to identify the students by basic mathematics tests and instruct them on their instructional levels. The learning differences of the students in each class must be similar. No top, middle and low students should be in the same class. With the units similar, students who have mastered a skill can help others who are having difficulty with a skill. The whole instructional period can be on every student's units in the homogeneous classroom.

In middle and high school, students who are on the same levels can be grouped together regardless of their grades. By checking students on basic mathematics, the teacher is helping them to become successful in every future math skill. The teacher must make success unavoidable for all students by teaching those on the same units together, regardless of their grade.

In the past students who were weak in these subjects were promoted, and many of them were never brought up to grade level in these subjects. This accounts for the very low national test scores in these subjects.

Together teachers can make a tremendous improvement by identifying those in middle and high schools who are not proficient and giving them the skills to accomplish good work in the remaining days in school. This is a cost effective way to correct a major problem until the elementary school students come to teachers prepared to handle middle and high school level work. National test scores will reveal that teachers are doing a tremendous job of educating students.

CHAPTER 19

THE IMPORTANCE OF ENGLISH BEING THE MAIN LANGUAGE IN OUR SCHOOLS

America has been a melting pot for all, and whoever desired to succeed. Americans should be adamant about their stance on elementary education, allowing no prejudice on the basis of race, religion, sex, ability or disability. All students should have the same opportunity to get an education that will prepare them to function for the benefit of society. Students that experience failure in a subject or grade should not suffer with a stigma that they cannot learn. Students can learn if they have teachers who will have goals to make success unavoidable for all students. The elementary school is the place where students pass elementary subjects. To do this, students need to know the English language.

A way to help make learning easier for teachers teaching language arts is to have students that are very similarly placed in groups that are closely related. For example, having language arts teachers teaching levels/units that are touching; such as, levels 5, 6 and 7.

Students that are on these levels in the same classrooms can benefit more than being in classrooms where the levels are 3, 6 and 8. When the subject matter being presented is more closely related, each student will benefit more from the material covered, especially if the students did not fully understand the concept when it was first presented. Additionally, there are students in the class who can assist other students who are having a problem learning the subject matter.

If students are promoted to a higher grade and do not complete the important material in the previous textbooks, gaps will be formed in their education. If this happens year after year, the missing material may result in lower test scores during the following years in school. Teachers should plan their curriculum in order to cover the important material in each textbook.

Teachers should speak distinctly, give the sense of what is said and help the students to understand material that is being presented. All students will be glad when they can understand the material that is presented to them.

Teachers should not be in a classroom just to collect a check every two weeks or once a month. They are paid by the school to teach students. If they are unable to do that they should not be in the classroom. That may sound bold for one to say, but each student must be taught by teachers who care for their students and are qualified to teach the subjects assigned to them in such a way that students will learn.

English must be taught so that every student will learn the language of America. The fringe benefit is that they will be able to help members of their households to learn to speak and read English also. America has been a melting pot, welcoming people from other language groups to live here. The schools can help these families to learn English through the students. There are many homes where English is not the language spoken in the home. People need to know English in order to communicate outside the home, get a job and speak when emergency situations arise.

A person who came to America many years ago, retired and lived in a community that spoke her native language. Due to the death of her husband, she moved in with family members who lived many miles away, and she had to have surgery. The facility did not have anyone on staff who knew the language and said they could not board her. This person had been in this country for over fifty years. If one of her children or someone else had taught her to speak English, she would have had no problem being treated in a facility designed to meet her physical needs at a critical time in her life.

There is no problem with other languages being taught in American schools. Many schools have added foreign languages to their curriculum. French, Spanish, German, Portuguese, Chinese, Japanese are just a few foreign languages found in our schools. It all depends on where one lives and the people groups that live in the area. People live in a world that has opened up to everyone, and learning different languages is possible through the entire years one is in elementary, middle and high schools. It would be wonderful having students learning foreign languages while they are in the elementary, middle and high schools.

Having students in the homerooms whose first language is not English, gives them the opportunity of sharing their native language with the class. However, English must be taught as the primary language in all schools. Many schools have ESL teachers for students who do not have English as their main language. The schools can meet an urgent need in many communities by using English to meet the language needs of students' families. It is using English as an asset to the community.

CHAPTER 20

THE IMPORTANCE OF HOME VISITS

By Deena Epps Fogle, B.A., M.Ed., Teacher of Year, 2012-2013

While many educators may be afraid of the thought of making home visits, they will find that making them will open the door of opportunity for them as well as the students they teach. What better way to get to know your students than to visit in their home environment?

Many educators are unaware of the cultural differences, economic hardships, and unique family dynamics that make up most homes in today's society. Yet they are not hesitant when it comes to assigning at–home projects in which they expect all students will have parents who will help them. Many parents may not be able to help. There are students who cannot succeed with this type of assignment.

Homes in which English is not the first language, homes in which students are in grave poverty, and homes in which there is not a family unit will be less able to ensure that students are successful.

Schools should require teachers and administrators to periodically make home visits in groups of two or three. These visits should be scheduled with the parents and have a positive goal in mind in order to gain more parental support and ensure the family-school connection. The suggestion of going in groups of two or three teachers is due to the fact that the family may have students that have other teachers. By several teachers who have students in the same neighborhoods going at the same time will assure parents of the interest the school has in their students. At least one visit in the fall and one in the spring would be good. In some cases, more visits may be needed depending on the needs of the family. Many students do not have sufficient food or garments. There are many schools that are meeting these situations with community assistance.

Teachers and administrators who break down the stigma relating to home visits in order to get to know their students' needs will have more caring classrooms in which the students can thrive educationally.

SECTION 5
CONCLUSIONS
(CHAPTERS 21-23)

CHAPTER 21

TEACHING TO MAKE SUCCESS UNAVOIDABLE FOR STUDENTS AND TEACHERS

Revolutionizing education by making success in learning language arts and mathematics unavoidable in the elementary school in grades one through five should be the goal of every elementary school.

These are goals that can be reached if educating students is the main reason for the existence of the school.

For Elementary School Students

The average students make it through school with little or no problems. Everything seems to suit them well. They have little boredom or frustrations. The type of students who seem to have problems in the elementary schools are the below-grade and above-grade level students.

It is the below-average and the above-average students that seem to have the most difficult time at school. The below-grade-level students who are promoted due to social promotion never seem to catch up with their receiving grade students. They are frustrated and end up at the bottom of the class, and this follows them all the way through school for the most part. If they make it to high school, it usually takes five years to graduate.

The above-grade-level students are faced with boredom. They usually find something else to do. This can lead them into trouble. The teacher has to stop to get their attention, send them to the office, or punish them some other way.

One big advantage of the AUG Plan for both below-grade and above-grade level students is their instructional needs are met by how they are taught on their instructional levels in homogeneous classrooms during language arts and basic mathematics. All students move at their own rate, and they are placed with students who are on the same units. During the time they are in the class, the teacher is spending the whole instructional time for them. They do not have to divide their time with students who are on different levels.

This arrangement can be followed because every teacher in the school is teaching language arts during the two period reading block. They are all teaching basic mathematics during the one period mathematics block. Students simply go to the teachers who are teaching their subjects.

This means that no teacher has to teach a class in which there are many different learning levels present in these subjects. All the students get the full period of instruction on their level. And best of all, the students in the class are all average students. There are no below-level or above-level students present. Everyone feels good because the class is organized for their maximum learning. The classes are taught by happy teachers making success unavoidable for each student.

Sometimes the teacher may have students who mastered a skill help students who are having a problem understanding the skill. It is a win-win situation for all in the class. The results from the AUG Plan benefit both the students and the teachers:

• First, almost every student will be reading on grade level by the end of grade five.

• Second, almost every student will master basic mathematics before going into the middle school.

• Third, almost every student will be ready for sixth grade. Why does one say "almost?" Because of Murphy's Law. There will almost, always be at least one to change the odds.

For Elementary School Teachers

• First, teachers will not have to teach many different levels each day in their language arts and basic mathematics classrooms.

• Second, teachers can teach the same units every year, if they desire to do so.

• Third, they will have all students on the levels they are teaching, thus less discipline problems.

• Fourth, teachers will be able to make success unavoidable.

For Middle and High School Students

Students who are not on grade level in language arts and/or basic mathematics can go to classrooms in the middle school and high school where their levels of language arts and basic mathematics are being taught. As soon as they are on grade level, they have completed their requirements and will move on to grade level work.

For Middle and High School Teachers

• First, teachers will receive students who are grade-level ready to learn in the homerooms. There will be no situation where grade level teachers will have to finish tasks that were to be completed the previous year.

• Second, teachers will be teaching students on their instructional levels in classrooms. All students in the class will be average students. Does that sound like fairy tales or dream situations for teachers that will never exist? The AUG Plan corrects the problems that existed when no adequate plans were in place to teach students who were below grade levels in language arts and basic mathematics. All the problems will not be solved overnight. But the elementary school is the place to begin. It may take years to bring students in middle and high schools to the place where they are on-grade level in reading and are prepared to handle middle and high school maths.

If the elementary students do not meet these goals, they will go to the middle school and be taught at their instructional levels in language arts and basic mathematics until they have mastered the skills. The middle school should have classes in reading and basic mathematics that will teach these students how to read and pass math on their grade level. In order for the AUG Plan to be effective, several plans have to be put into place.

• First, language arts must be taught in a two period block at the same time every day in grades 1–5. Mathematics must be taught in a one period class at the same time every day in grades 1–5 during the mornings, preferably right after reading/language arts. The subjects taught in the homerooms can be taught at the discretion of each homeroom teacher after language arts and mathematics are taught. Music, art, and physical education classes will be based on the schedules of the specialists.

• Second, all teachers may have up to a maximum of three reading units preparations of touching levels and up to two mathematics preparations for an instructional day. They can teach the same units and levels every year if they so desire.

• Third, all students must go to the teachers who are teaching their levels. This may mean some students would remain in their homerooms, some would go to other teachers on grade level, some may have to go down a grade level if their instructional levels were not taught on their grade levels; and some may have to go up a grade level in order to be taught on their instructional levels.

• Fourth, students would have to master each unit before moving on to the next. When a level is completed, they would go to the teachers who teach their new levels.

• Fifth, the rooms for language arts and basic mathematics are integrated, homogeneous classrooms, and all students are placed according to their abilities to be taught on their instructional levels until they are able to read independently and/or know their basic mathematics.

• Sixth, the students are ability grouped only in these subjects, and when the periods are over, they return to their integrated, heterogeneous homerooms to be taught the other subjects on grade level. They are in homogeneous classes for only three periods a day.

• Seventh, English is the main means of communicating in America, language arts gives students the foundation for using English as the main form of communication. All students in the elementary school should learn to use the language effectively

The purposes of the Plan are to:

• Set up the ideal learning environment for all teachers and students,

• Make the teaching of students more effective in homerooms and classrooms,

• Treat all students fairly to insure that all know how to read and master basic mathematics in order for them to be successful in all their future education.

These must be the purposes for the existence of the elementary schools. The AUG Plan provides ways to:

• Treat all students without discrimination,

• Give all teachers a plan that will allow them to be successful in teaching,

• Make success in learning unavoidable for all students.

CHAPTER 22

THE COST EFFECTIVE AND EFFICIENT WAY TO EDUCATE ALL STUDENTS

There is a cost effective and efficient way to educate all students. A school is not properly educating elementary school students if they cannot read on grade level, master basic mathematics and know the English language before they move on to middle school.

These three main goals cannot be achieved without having an organizational plan that will result in students being:

• 1. Taught to read on their instructional levels,

• 2. Taught to master basic mathematics and

• 3. Taught to fully use the English language.

The schools must make sure there are no educational gaps in student learning as they move from grade to grade. This can be done only by having a plan that results in making success unavoidable in these three areas for all students.

The AUG Plan was designed to achieve these goals. It was tried and found successful. I was principal of Marshall Elementary School in Orangeburg, South Carolina from 1978 to 1982. My first year there I had to place over 500 students in grades K to 5. I was given the information on each student–name, address, reading unit/level, math unit/level and grade. As I looked at the data, I noticed many levels in reading and math that needed to be taught in each grade. I knew no teachers could teach all these levels in their classrooms. It would be an impossible situation not only for the teachers but also for the students. All I could do was pray for wisdom to know how to help teachers and students in this situation. God answered that prayer and gave me the ideas for the AUG Plan.

Students had to have basic mathematics and language arts taught in each grade at the same time in order to be able to go to the teachers who were teaching their unit/level in homogeneous classrooms. Teachers would make success unavoidable for all students in this setting. They would have the other grade level subjects taught in heterogeneous homerooms. Every student would be properly educated with no gaps in learning.

There was to be no difference in homerooms. All grade levels would have the same composition of students to be a replica of the community in which they lived. As students learned to work together in the homeroom, they could model that behavior back in the community. Teachers would enjoy teaching because the learning environment would be ideal for student learning. The students would have more instructional time in this setting.

When the plan was presented to the faculty, I made it clear if the plan did not work we would go back to the old system. I have learned when one makes changes, it is best to present it this way. Needless to say, the teachers were pleased with the results. Students were happy and were making good progress in their education.

I had one parent who opposed the change in September, 1978. I told her the same as I told the staff. It is interesting she had a student in third grade who had to go to second grade because first grade level language arts was not being taught on third grade. Students had to go to the teachers who were teaching their levels, whether it was on grade level, above grade level, or below grade level. This was true for both classroom subjects. After the classes were over they returned to their homerooms.

In March, 1980, the student was in fifth grade, reading on grade level. His mother came to school the day he was on grade level and thanked me for the AUG Plan. Her son was the one I saw years later after he finished high school carrying a paperback book in his back pocket. He learned to read when the AUG Plan required him to go to second grade. But because all students were moving to the teachers teaching their levels, no peers knew where he went. When he saw there were students in second grade who were reading, he quickly learned to read on a level that was taught in third grade.

Regarding basic mathematics, a parent recently told me her grandson, who was a good reader in fourth grade, was having problems in basic mathematics because he never learned his multiplication tables. The teacher told the student he did not have to memorize the multiplication tables. If a student does not master each skill in basic mathematics, that student will not be able to handle middle and high school math. Many middle and high school teachers will tell everyone that the reason students are having problems in math today is because they have not mastered counting, addition and subtraction, division and multiplication, fractions or measurements. All future mathematics are built on the foundation of basic mathematics. The teacher was wrong saying that to the student. He will not be able to do middle and high schools math without knowing the multiplication tables. Daniel who wrote chapter 16 is a high school math teacher. Every year he has a few students who do not know basic mathematics. They cannot handle high school math.

One thing that we are facing in education today is that many students are not on grade level. Throwing money at the problem is not the solution. One school district spent $3 million for "the Voyager program to bring students up to grade level in English, language arts and math."[89] Do you realize how many teachers could be employed teaching students for one year with that amount of money? If a beginning certified teacher earns $25,000 a year, $3 million will pay for 120 teachers. If experienced teachers earn $35,000 a year that same amount will hire just over 85 teachers.

Another school district is paying the Common Core Institute $127,000 for a professional development training program.[90] Using the above figures that would hire 5 teachers at $25,000 or 3.5 teachers at $35,000. All of that can be wasted money. Remember all certified teachers in the elementary schools are trained to teach students language arts and basic mathematics. They have not been trained to teach students how to take state tests. What are many of these teachers doing? Teaching students to take state tests that are no indicators of what students need to know to live in our society. Schools are not organized in an efficient or effective way to assure that all students can read on grade level and master basic mathematics, which are the foundational subjects upon which to build one's education.

Social promotion is a failure because students are promoted with learning gaps that are never fully removed by the present educational system. There are no plans to effectively bring these students up to grade level in language arts and basic mathematics when they are sent up a grade unprepared to handle the subject matter. The way to stop the gaps is to teach all students on their instructional levels in reading and basic mathematics in the elementary schools where teachers are able to educate them. The AUG Plan explains how it can be done in a cost effective and efficient way. We have provided the plan. Now it is up to the leadership of the elementary schools to put it into effect. If it is not done, the students will suffer the most. The test scores will continue to be low. Schools will continue to waste taxpayer's money. The problems will not be solved by more money. Only a new organizational plan can solve the problem, and it will not cost more money. Students will not be able to pass the exit exams unless adequately prepared.

CHAPTER 23

DEFINITION OF TERMS

All students – should be taught with their age mates on grade level in heterogeneous homerooms. However, in language arts and basic mathematics, students should be taught on their instructional levels in homogeneous classes.

AUG Plan – a structured organizational plan for grades one through five in the elementary schools that enables students to be placed in heterogeneous homerooms for homeroom subjects and in homogeneous classrooms for instruction in language arts and basic mathematics, making success unavoidable for all students.

AYP – "Adequate Yearly Progress" is the goal set for the total school population of schools receiving funds under Title One. If the goals are not met, funding can be lost for those schools.

Boredom – that which is uninteresting or dull and causes students not to pay full attention.

Charter Schools – independent public schools allowed freedom to be more innovative, while being held accountable for improved student achievement. They foster a partnership between parents, teachers and students to create an environment in which parents can be more involved, teachers are given the freedom to innovate, and students are provided the structure they need to learn, with all three being held accountable for improved student achievement.

Classroom Level Subjects – language arts and basic mathematics are taught on instructional levels in homogenous classrooms. Students go to the teachers who are teaching their levels.

Eighty per cent mastery – students having 8 out of 10 answers correct before moving on to the next skill/unit.

Frustration – that which is beyond one's instructional level and causes one to feel unable to handle the subject matter adequately.

Grade Promotion – students are promoted each year to the next grade in heterogeneous homerooms where they are taught grade level subjects. They are taught language arts and basic mathematics in homogeneous classrooms on their instructional levels.

Handicap students – handicap students are to be mainstreamed and placed with their age-mates whenever possible. They will be taught on their instructional levels in language arts and basic mathematics. Their IEP must show placement in a grade level heterogeneous homeroom.

Heterogeneous grouping – all teachers will form heterogeneous groups within their homerooms composed of top, middle and low level students. Every group will have at least one student who is on grade level in reading and one who is on grade level in basic mathematics.

Heterogeneous homerooms – placing students together in grade level homerooms comprised of students who have a wide range of instructional levels. All grade level homerooms are identical in composition.

Home visits – the practice of teachers making visits to the homes of their students to communicate how well the students are doing in school. Teachers can go by twos in making home visits. The other teacher can teach another grade and have students in the same area.

Homeroom Roll Form A – used at the end of the school year by homeroom teachers to give the data on each student for placement for the next school year.

Homeroom Roll Form B – is used by the one setting up the homerooms for enrollment in the next school year.

Homeroom Subjects – these are the grade level subjects taught in heterogeneous homerooms: art, health, music, physical education, science and social studies.

Homerooms – all are heterogeneous and are organized the same way except preschool and first grade, which may not have reading or math scores to use in placement.

Homogeneous classroom – placing students together in classrooms where all students are on the same level in the same subject. The subjects are either language arts or basic mathematics.

How students arrive at school: Bus – the students that arrive at school on the school bus or other bus. Car pool – the students that arrive at school by car or van. Walk – the students that arrive at school by walking.

IEP – "Individualized Educational Plan" is prepared for a student based on the student's needs. All special education students must have an IEP.

Instructional levels – levels of learning in language arts or basic mathematics where success is unavoidable. Students are instructed in homogeneous classes on their learning levels with students on the same levels. No one is above or below students in this setting. All students are average students in the homogeneous classrooms.

Integrated homerooms – students from various environments learning to work together in the same environment, ultimately carrying over into their neighborhoods.

Mastery of units or levels – students must reach 80% or higher mastery on a unit test or level test before moving on to the next unit or level in language arts and basic mathematics. That is 8 or more right answers for every 10 questions.

Multiracial – an integrated group of students on grade level representing all of the students on that grade level in homerooms.

No Child Left Behind – (NCLB) a federal law that requires school districts to bring students up to the proficient level on state tests by the end of the school year. It represents legislation that attempts to accomplish standard-based educational reform.

Parent Trigger Law – passed in 2010, allows the majority of parents of a chronically under-performing school to petition to overhaul staff and curriculum or to turn the school into a charter school.

Peter/Paul effect – teachers assisting one group of students at the expense of the other groups. In an average classroom, a teacher may give more instructional time for the below-average students than to the other students or give more instructional time to the above average students than to the rest of the class.

Pupils – all students should be taught grade level subjects with their age-mates on grade level in heterogeneous homerooms, with the exception of language arts and basic mathematics being taught in homogeneous classrooms to students on the same instructional levels.

Social promotion – promoting a student from one grade level to the next higher grade level on the basis of age rather than academic achievement. This is good only if their language arts and basic mathematics needs are met in homogeneous classrooms where their instructional levels are being taught.

Standard deviation—a statistical term for the distance + or - from the mean.

With the bell shaped curve, 100 is the mean. One standard deviation – or + from mean is 85 or 115 IQ. For two sd, - or + would be 70 or 130 IQ.

Teachers – those who are state certified and have current credentials showing that they are fully qualified to teach their assigned subjects to their students.

Touching levels – what is before and what is after; an example is 6, 7, 8 and not 4, 7, 10. The purpose for teaching touching levels is to keep the ability range within the classroom very similar. No one in the class is way above or way below the rest of the class. The teacher in this setting can be effective in making success for every student unavoidable. It is primarily for the elementary school plan but is excellent for all grades in schools where students are below grade level in language arts and/or basic mathematics.

ABOUT THE AUTHOR

Frank H. Meyers is a longtime educator with experience in the public school system, Christian schools, churches, and at the college level. He has a Ph.D. in the areas of curriculum and instruction in the field of Early Childhood Education and M.Ed. from the University of Sourth Carolina, a M.R.E. and B.Th. from Southern Methodist College, a B.A. from Bob Jones University, and is an ordained Baptist pastor. He wrote "Teaching To Make Success Unavoidable In The Elementary School" because he has a desire to create a win-win plan for success for students, teachers, and administrators. Meyers currently resides in South Carolina with his wife Shirley. The couple has ten family members actively involved in teaching.

CONTRIBUTORS

Harry Graham Peters

Peters has a B.A. from the University of Western Ontario, and an M.Ed. from Florida Atlantic University. He's a retired elementary school teacher, and long-time friend to the author. He wrote "Rural Ungraded School."

Daniel Yiannakis Tittiris

Tittiris has a B.S from Bob Jones University, and an M.Ed. from Liberty University. He's a high school math teacher and the author's grandson. He was the Teacher of the year in 2011-12, at Chatham High School. He wrote "How To Teach Basic Mathematics."

Deena Epps Fogle

Fogle has a B.A. from Coker College, and an M.Ed. from Claflin University, ESOL (English to Speakers of Other Languages) teacher, 12 years, Orangeburg Consolidated School District 5, Teacher of the years 2012-13 Sheridan Elementary School. Fogle wrote "The Importance of Home Visits."

Jennifer Midgett Meyers

Meyers has a B.S. from Cumberland University. She's been an elementary school teacher for seven years, and is the author's daughter-in-law. She wrote "Basic Reading Instruction."

Stephanie Joy Tittiris

Tittiris is a university student and the author's granddaughter. She plans to be a special education teacher when she graduates. Stephanie took the picture on the cover.

Sheri Meyers Tittiris

Tittiris has a B.S. from Bob Jones University. She has been a third grade teacher for 25 years, and is the author's daughter. Sheri designed the cover.

ENDNOTES

All websites were accessed prior to 2014. You can access the same articles online by searching for the article's title and the author's name in your Internet search engine.

Introduction

1 "Notable students of one-room schools," (http://en.wikipedia.org/wiki/Ungraded-school).

Prologue

2 McGuffey, William Holmes. (*McGuffey Reader*,) 7 vol set. Mott Media, Inc. Milford, MI 48042, 1837.

Chapter 1

3 GreatSchoolsStaff, "High School exit exam: Issues to consider," (www.greatschools.org/students/academic-skills/587/-high-school-exit-exams-issues.gs). See: page 1, "What subjects are tested?"

4 Joanne Jacobs, "Honor Student fails graduation test," (www.Joanne-jacobs.com/tag/exit-exam).

5 Christine Armario, "12th grade still below '92 reading scores," (www.Go-erie.com/app5dll/article?a/d=2010 101118/apa/1011181237).

6 Robert Rosenthal and Lenore Jacobson, (*Pygmalian In The Classroom*), (Irvinging Publishers, Inc. 1968), pp.72-79.

7 Charles Thompson and Elizabeth Cunningham, "Retention and Social Promotion: Research and Implications for Policy," (www.Eric-aenet/eda/ed442941.htlm). See, "Findings From the Research."

8 Marybeth Sullivan, "Education Mandates On Local School Districts," (www.cga.ct.gov/2013/rpt/2013-r-0047.htm).

9 "Atlanta Public Schools May Have To Return Nearly $1 Million In Federal Funds," (www.huffingtonpost.com/2011/07/14/Atlanta-public school-ma-h 898330.html).

10 2009 Study by Universary of Chicago, CCRS, "Closing Schools: Why it's not a good idea," (http://seattleeducation2010.wordpress.com/2013/03/31/closing-schools-why-its-not-a-good-idea-2/0). See "CReATE Releases Research Brief on School Closures."

11 Monica Brady-Myerov, "Lawrence Public Schools Face Possible State Takeover," (www.wbur.org/2011/11/29/lawrence-schools-takeover).

12 2009 Study by Universary of Chicago. CCRS, "Closing Schools: Why it's not a good idea." (http://seattleeducation2010.wordpress.com/2013/03/31/closing-schools-why-its-not-a-good-idea-2/0). See "Racial Disparities of School Closings."

13 Mike Bostack and Kevin Quealy, "How The Chicago School Districts Compares," (www.nytimes.com/interctive/2012/09/14/us/how-the-chicago-public-district-compares.html?-r=0). See, "Recall Rights."

14 2009 Study by the University of Chicago, CCRS, op. cit. See "Racial Disparites of School Closings."

15 Bostack, op. cit. See, "Salary for B.A. and M.A."

16 "Chicago Public Schools lays off nearly 850 employees after closings approved," (www.foxnews.com/us/2013/06/15/chicago-/schools-announce-52m-in-cuts-layoffs/).

17 CReATE Research Brief #5 School Closures March 2013.pdf (www.dropbox.com/s/tq712v9x47gkajo/CReATE%20Research%20Brief%20%23)

5%20School%20Closures%20March%20213.pdf.)   See page 1, Under-performing schools.

18 Sarah Karp, "Losing Track," From Spring 2013 issue of Catalyst Chicago School Closings. (www.catalyst-chicago.org/news/2013/04/03/20943/losing-tract).

19 Mary Landrieu, "Louisiana Association of Public Charter Schools Louisiana leads the way on charter schools," (http://lacharter-schools.org/news-and-events/16-louisiana-leads-the-way-on-charter-schools-mary-landrieu). May 28, 2012.

20 Sarah Laskow, "Necessity Is The Mother of Invention," (www.the dailybeast.com/newsweek/2010/08/26/new-orleans-s-charter-school-revolution.html).

21 Ibid.

22 Public Schools, from Wikipedia, (http://en.wikipedia.org/wiki/public schools).

23 Charter Schools, "Center for Research on Education Outcomes, CCREDO," (http://en.wikipedia.org/wiki/charter_schools).

24 Carl Gibson, "Close Corporation Tax Loop Hole, Not Public Schools," (www.huntingtonpost.com/carl-gibson/close-corporate-tax b_2972688.html).

25 Joanne Jacobs, op. cit.

26 Sarah Laskow, op. cit.

Chapter 2

27 Lawren Allphin, "What Happens in Reading: Spring," (http://education.com/magazine/article.Kindergarten_Reading_Update Aprto June/).

28 Debra Viadero, "Study says most 1st grade classes not high quality," (hppt://education.com/reference/article/study-study-says-most-1st-grade-classes-not/).

29 Hope Yen and Christine Armario, "Language a barrier for Latinos in schools," (http://www.thebassbarn.com/forum/showthread.php?t=226474).

30 "Writing Now," (http:ncte.org/library/NCTEFiles/Resource/Policy Research/WrtgResearchBrief.pdf).

31 M. Ira Dubins, "Some Trends and Problems in Teaching Science in the Elementary School," (http//onlinelibrary.wiley.com/doi10.111/j.1949-8594.1957.tb08149.x/abstract).

32 Caroline Divine, "Science in Elementary Schools," Question # 3, (http://www.Divinecaroline.com/34/33707-science-elementary-schools).

33 Robert J Wallace, "Science in Elementary Schools," New York Univerdity, Math, Science and Technology (MSTEP). (www.divine caroline.com/34/33707/science-elementary-school).

34 Lynn Davey, "The Case for a National Testing System," (http://pareonline.net/getvn.asp?v=3&n=1).

Chapter 3

35 Valerie Strauss, "Leading mathematician debunks value added," The American Seat. Notice of the American Mathematics Society, May 9, 2011, (www.washingtonpost.com/blogs/answer-sheet/post leading-mathematician-debunks-value-added/201105/08/AFb999UG_blog.html).

36 Jamie Self, "SC plan to grade teachers stirs protests," (www.thestate.com/2012/12/26/2568261/sc-plan-to-grade-teachers-stirs.html).

37 Valerie Strauss, Op. Cit. See 4th paragraph under article by John Ewing.

38 Ibid.

39 Alan Judd and others. "Cheating Our Children; Suspect Scores Put Award's Integrity In Question." (www.ajc.com/news/local/cheating-our-children-suspect scores-put awards-integrity-nQTPY).

40 "School Trustees Question Use of Small Groups." *The Times and Democrat*, Orangeburg, South Carolina. October 20, 2012. pp. A1 & A3.

41 Donna Krache, "Parent Trigger Laws," (http://schoolsofthought.blogs.cnn.com/2012/03/14/five-minute-primer-parent-trigger-laws/).

Chapter 4

42 Lindsey Burke, "National Education Standards and Tests: Big Expense, Little Value." (www.heritage.org/research/reports/2011/02/national- education-standards-and-big-expense-little-value).

43 Lynn Davey, op. cit.

44 Valerie Strauss, "A Better way to evaluate students and schools," (www.fairtest.org/sites/default/files/better ways to evaluate schools factsheet.pdf), see under Large-scale tests.

45 M. B. Pell, "Major cheating scandals inevitable, as states can't ensure test integrity," (www.ajc.com/news/more-cheating-scandals-inevitable-as-states-cant-e/nSPqj/).

46 Heather Vogell, and others, "Cheating our children: suspicious school test scores across the nation," (www.ajc.com/news/more-cheating-scandals-inevitable-inevitable-as-states-cant-e/).

47 "Duncan: Feds 'Looking At' Cheating In Atlanta," (www.huffing-ton-post.com/2011/07/18/duncan-feds-looking-at-ch-n-901837.html).

48 Bill Turque, "Henderson asks inspector general to investigate test erasures," (http://articles.washingtonpost.com/2011-03-29/local/352608201-erasures-caveon-test-security-answer-sheets).

49 Paul E. Peterson and others, "U.S. Proficiency in Math and Reading Lags Behind That of Most Industrial Nations, Endangering Long Term Economic Growth," (http://educationnext.org/u -s-profic-ieny-in-math-and-reading-lags-behind-that-0f-most-industrial-nations-endangering-long-term-economic-growth/).

50 "No Child Left Behind Waivers Granted to 33U.S. States, Some Attached With Strings," (www.huffingtonpost.com/2012/07/19/no-child-left-behind-waiver_n_1684504.html).

51 "Another Casualty: The Taxpayer." Fourth heading under article "What is Diploma Choice" at (http://diplomachoice.com).

52 Copy taken from a 1950 high school College Entrance Diploma

from the state of New York to a graduating senior. See New York
State University Regents College Entrance Diploma. (http://en.
wiki.pedia.org/wiki/Regents-Examinations).

Chapter 5

53 "Students At and Above Grade Level For Reading In Grade 3
Graduate From High School At Higher Rates Than Students Below Grade
Level". (www. chapinhall.org/research/inside-students-and-above-grade-
level-reading-grade-3-graduates-high-school-higher-rates-stu).

54 Charles Thompson and Elizabeth Cunningham. op. cit., See Findings
from the research.

55 "Why More Standardized Tests Won't Improve Education." (http://
parents-acrossamerica.org/why-standardized-tests-won't-improve-education).

Chapter 7

56 "Academic Self-Concept," Look under "Self -Concept," (http://en.
wikipedia.org/wiki/self-concept). See footnote 17.

57 "Early Warning! Why Reading by the End of Third Grade Matters,"
(www.aecf.org/-/media/Pubs/Initiatives/KIDS%20COUNT/123/
2010KCSpecReport/Special%20Report%20Executive%20Summary.pdf),
page 2.

58 Ibid., page 1.

59 Matthew 7:12, NIV.

60 D. H. Granello and J.P. Granello, "Suicide Risk In Children,"
(http//www.education.com/reference/article/suicide-rick-children/).

61 Akiko Fujita, "Kids and Laughing Teachers Bullied Suicide

Teen" (http://abcnews.go.com/blogs/headlines/2012/07/kids-and-laughing-teachers-bullied-teen/).

Chapter 8

62 "Social promotion," Wikipedia Encyclopedia (http:wikipedia.org/wiki/Social Promotion).

63 Elissa Gootman, "Social promotion will end in 5th, grade, Mayor says," (www.nytimes.com/2004/09/10/education/10school.html).

64 Howard Blume, " Los Angeles schools to revamp their ban on social promotion, (http://articles.latimes.com/2011/jul/18/local/la-me-laud-promote-20110718.)

65 Gootman, op. cit. See, paragraph eleven.

66 J. Aldridge and R. Goldman, "Social Promotion," (www.education.com/reference/article/social-promotion-education/). See pages 1 and 2.

67 Gootman, op. cit. See, Social promotion will end....

68 Aldridge and Goldman, op. cit., page 2.

69 "Research Spotlight on Academic Ability Grouping," (www.nea.org/tools/16899.htm).

70 "Ability Grouping," definition from Wikipedia Encyclopedia, (http://en.wikipedia.org/wiki/abilitygrouping).

Chapter 9

71 "Printable Dolch Sight Word List." (http://bogglesworldesl.com/dolch lists.htm).

Chapter 10

72 Rick Desloge, "Jimmie Edwards: Innovative Concept Academy," *St. Louis Business Journal*, September 9, 2011.

73 "Eleven Facts About Dropping Out," (www. dosomething.org/tips andtools/11-facts-about-dropping-out#).

74 Rosenthral, op. cit. Pages 72-79.

75 Dale Linder-Altman, "District Tries New Approach For Behavior." *The Times And Democract*, Orangeburg, South Carolina. September 25, 2012. p. A4.

76 Martha Rose Brown, "District 3 hires 34 new teachers, with more than half 'fresh out of college,'" *The Times and Democrat*, Orangeburg, South Carolina,August, 17, 2013, page A2.

77 "Students At and Above Grade Level for Reading in Grade 3 Graduate from High School at Higher Rates Than Students Below Grade Level". op. cit.

78 Printable Dolch Sight Word List, op. cit.

Chapter 12

79 Carl Friedrich Guass, (http://en.wikipedia.org/wiki/carl_ friedrich_guass).

80 Normal distribution, (http://en.wikipedia.org/wili/normal distribution).

81 C. George Boeree, *Intelligence and IQ*, Shippensburg University, Shippensburg, PA 17257. page 6.

82 Ibid., "Bell shape curve of normal distribution based on student's IQ."

83 Robert Rosenthal and Lenore Jacobson. *Pygmalian In The Class-room*, Irvington Publishers, Inc., New York, 1992, 1968. pp. 72-79.

84 Chang, Jie, "A Case Study of the 'Pygmalian Effect:' Teacher Expection and Student Achievement," (www.google.com/search/client=safari&ris=en&q=Pygmalion+in+the+classroom+by+Rosenthaul&ie=UTF-&&oe=UTF-8).

Chapter 15
85 Mick Zais, "S.C. NAEP math, reading scores unchanged; below national average," *The Times And Democrat,* Orangeburg, South Carolina, November 2, 2011, page A2.

86 Daniel Y Tittiris is the author of chapter 17.

Chapter 17
87 Printable Dolch Sight Word List, op. cit.

Chapter 18
88 Ibid.

Chapter 22
89 Linder, "District 5 tries new approach for behavior". Op. Cit., Page A3.

90 Brown, Op. Cit. Page A2.

BIBLIOGRAPHY

A. BOOKS

Beadle, Muriel. *A Child's Mind.* Doubleday & Company, Inc. 1970.

Boeree, C. George. *Intelligence and IQ.* Shippensburg University, Shippensburg, PA, 27257.

Carson, Ben. *Gifted Hands.* Zonderran Publishing House, 1991, 1990.

Laird, Charlton. *Webster's New World Thesaurus.* Simon & Schuster, Inc. New York, 2003.

McGuffey, William Holmes. *McGuffey Reader,* 7 vol set. Mott Media, Inc. Milford, MI 48042, 1837.

Rosenthal, Robert and Lenore Jacobson. *Pygmalian In The Classroom.* Irvington Publishers, Inc., New York, 1992, 1968.

Webster's New World Dictionary: Basic School Edition. The Southwestern Company, Nashville, 1971.

B. NEWSPAPERS, JOURNALS AND PERIODICALS

Adcox, Seanna. "S.C. SAT scores fall again, passing AP scores up." *The Times And Democract,* Orangeburg, South Carolina. September 25, 2012. p. A4.

Aldridge, J. and Goldman, R. "Alternatives to Social Promotion and Grade Retention." (www. education.com/reference/article/

alternatives-Social-promotion-retention/2page=2).

_____."Social Promotion." See page 2c, "Conclusions about Social Promotion," page 2c. (www.education,com/reference/article/grade-retention/?page=3).

_____."Social Promotion." See 2b,"Implications and Findings from Local Social Promotion Policies." (www.education.com/reference/article/social-promotion-education/).

_____."Social Promotion." See page 2a, "Negative Effects of Social Promotion," page 2a, (www.education.com/reference/article/social-promotion-education/).

_____."Social Promotion." See page 1, "Prevalence of social promotion." (www.education.com/reference/article/social-promotion-education/).

Allpin, Lawren. "What Happens In K Reading:Spring." (http:www.education.com/magazine/article/k-r-u-Apr-to-June/?page=2).

Badertscher, Nancy. "Major cheating scandals inevitable, as states can't ensure test integrity." *The Atlanta Journal-Constitution*. September 30, 2012.

"Bell shape curve." Table from Intelligence, Vol 24, No 1. January-Febuary, 1997.

"Bill could hike charter school number in S. C." *The Times and Democrat*, March 16, 2012, p. A6.

Brandon, Craig, "The Five Year Party" *The Atlanta Journal Constitution*, *Atlanta*. July 8, 2011.

Burton, Lynsi. "Solving middle school problems in elementary School."

(www.bremertonpatriot.com/news/10292125.html).

Davidson, Helen. "Ability Grouping." (http://www.education.com/reference/article/ability-grouping/).

Desloge, Rick. "Jimmie Edwards: Innovative Concept Academy." *St. Louis Business Journal*, September 9, 2011.

Dillon, Sam. "Sluggish Results Seen In Math Scores." (www.nytimes.com/2009/10/15/education/15math.html). October, 14, 2009.

_____."Study compares American students with other countries," (www.nytimes.com/2007/11/15/world/americas/5ith-14students.8345918.htm).

Dubins, M. Ira. "Some Trends and Problems in TeachingScience." (http://onlinelibrary.willey.com/doi/10.1111/j.1949-8594.1957.tb08149.x/abstract).

Duncan, Arne. "Feds Looking At Cheating In Atlanta." *The Atlanta Journal Constitution*, July 18, 2012.

Gootman, Eilissa. "Social Promotion Will End In 5th Grade, Mayor Says." *New York Times*, September 18, 2011."

Granello, D. H. and Granello, J.P. "Suicide Risk In Children." (http//www.education.com/reference/article/suicide-rick-children/).

"Grouping Kids By Ability Harms Education, Two Studies Show" *Science Daily*. September 15, 2007.

Hentoff, Nat. "School to prison pipeline." *The Times And Democract*, Orangeburg, South Carolina. March 16, 2012, p. A7.

Isenese, Laura. "More FCAT 2.0 results released for reading, math and science." (www.miamiherald.com/2012/06/04/2833798/morefcat-20-results-released.html).

Jones, Rodger M. "Open rebellion against school test in Texas." (rm.jones @dallasnews,com) February 14, 2012.

Kohn, Alfie. "Standardized Testing is here to stay." *Education Week*, September 27, 2000.

Layton, Lyndsey and Brown, Emma. "SAT Reading Scores Hit a Four-Decade Low." (washingtonpost.com/local/education/sat-reading-scores-hit-a-four-decade-low/2012/09/24/7ec9cble-0643-11e2-afff-d6c7f20a836f_story.html).

Leckrone, M. J. and Griffin, B.G. "Retention realities and educational standards." (http://www.redorbit.com/news/education/357610/retention-realities-and-educational-standards).

Linder-Altman, Dale. "District Tries New Approach For Behavior." *The Times And Democract*, Orangeburg, South Carolina. September 25, 2012. p. A4.

_____. "Region's end-of-course testing better, but history's a problem,'" *The Times And Democract*, Orangeburg, South Carolina. October 15, 2012. p. A2.

_____. "SAT scores up locally ." *The Times And Democract*, Orangeburg, South Carolina. October 15, 2012. p. A3.

_____. "School Trustees Question Use of Small Groups." *The Times and Democract*, Orangeburg, South Carolina. October 20, 2012. pp. A1 & A3.

Nagaoka, Jenny and Roderick, Melissa. "Ending Social Promotion: The Effects of Retention." (http://ccsr.uchicago.edu/publications/ending-social-promotion-effects-retention).

"No Child Left Behind Waivers Granted to 33 U.S. States, Some Attached With Strings." (http://www.huffingtonpost.com/2012/07/19/no-child-left-behind-waiver_n_1684504.html).

Parnos, Sarah. "Tests show students struggle to explain answers." *Associate Press*, June 19, 2012.

"S. C. NAEP math, reading scores unchanged below national average." *The Times and Democrat*, November 2, 2011, p. A2.

"6 Reasons to Rethink Standardized Tests" (http://tamris908.edublogs.org/2012/02/08/6-reasons-to-rethink-standardized-test/).

"Social Promotion = Academic Failure." (www.societyforqualityeducation.org/index.php/blog/read/social-promotion-academic-failure/).

Strass, Valerie. "A better way to evaluate students and schools," (//voices.washingtonpost.com/answer-sheet/standardized-tests/a-better-wait-to-evaluate-stude.html).

_____. "Leading mathematician debunks 'value added,'" The American Seat. Notice of the American Mathematics Society, May 9, 2011. (www.washingtonpost.com/blogs/answer-sheet/post/leading-mathematician-debunks-value-added/2011/05/08/AFb999UG_blog.html).

Thomas, Evans and Wingert, Pat. "Why We Must Fire Bad Teachers" (www.thedailybeast.com/newsweek/2010/03/05/why-we-must-fire-bad-teachers.html).

"US Proficiency in Math and Reading Lags Behind That of Most Indus-
trialized Nations, Endangering Long Term Economic Growth."
(http:educationnext.org/u-s-proficienty-in-math-nd-reading-lags-
industrializednations-endangering-long-behind-that-of-most-term-
economic-growth/).

Viadero, Debra. "Study Says Most 1st Grade Classes Not High Quality."
(www.education.com/reference/article/study-says-most-1st-g-re
classes-not/).

Vogell, Heather, and others."Cheating our children: suspicious school
test scores across the nation." *The Atlanta Journal-Constitution.*
March, 25, 2012.

"Writing Now." (http://www.ncte.org/liberty/NCTEFiles/Resorce/Policy
Research/WrtgResearch Brief.pdf).

Zais, Mick. "Too little known about presidents, civic matters" (http://the
tandd.com/news/matters-too-little—known-about-presidents-civic-
matters_1d53do36-59f6-oo471.e3ce6c.html). February 20, 2012.

_____. "Modernize school, educator accountability." *The Times And
Democract.* Orangeburg, South Carolina. March 28, 2012, p. A8.

_____."Bill could hike charter school number in S.C." *The Times And
Democract,* Orangeburg, South Carolina. March 16, 2012. p. A8.

C. OTHER SOURCES

"Ability Grouping." Definition. (http://wn.wikipedia.org/wiki/ability
grouping).

"Academic Self-Concept." Look under "Self -Concept," See footnote 17 (http://en.wikipedia.org/wiki/self-conctep).

Altman, Lynda. "The problem with standardized tests" (http://voices.ya-hoo.com/the-problems-standardized-tests-7812310,html?cat4).

_____. "Are U.S. Schools at Their Breaking Point?" (http://voices. Yahoo.com/are-us-schools-their-breaking-point-8763379.html).

"Another Casualty: The Taxpayer." #3 Heading under article #1 "What is Diploma Choice" at (http://diplomachoice.com).

Armario, Christine. "Wake up call: U.S. Students trail global leaders." (www.msmbc.msn.com/ld/40544897/ns/us/news-life/t/wake-up call-us-sudents-trail-gltobal-leaders/#.,UGkkF461/lSV) December 7, 2010.

_____. "More states defying federal gov't on education law." (www.sf-examiner,com/news/2012/2/01/state-higher-education-spending-sees-big-decline-07 category=18).

_____. "State higher education speeding sees big decline." (www.sfexaminer.com/news/2012/2/01/state-higher-education-spending-sees-big-decline-07 category=18).

_____. "12th grade students still below '92 reading scores." (www.go-erie.com/app5dll/article?a/d=2010 101118/apa/1011181237).

Braddock, Jamills Henry and Slavin, Robert J."Why Ability Grouping must end: Achieving Excellence & Equity in American Education. ERIC EJ466357.

"Big Cities Battle Dismal Graduation Rates" (www.cbsnews.com/stories/

2008/04/0/national/main3986714.shtml).

Brooks, Robert. '"How Can Teachers Foster Self-Esteem in Children?" (www.greatschools.org/special-education/health/773-teachers-foster-self-esteem-in-children.gs).

Brown, Travis H and Rachel Keller Brown. "A Brave New Education For St Louis Public Schools and Judge Jimmie Edwards." (www.pe-lopidas.com/philanthropy/brave-education-sr-louis-public).

Burke, Lindsey. "National Education Standards and Tests: Big Expense, Little Value." (www.heritage.org/research/reports/2011/02/national-education-standards-and-big-expense-little-value).

"Common Discipline Problems of Elementary School Children and How to Deal with them." The Parent Institute, Fairfax Station, VA 22039, 2004. (One of a series of Parent Guides).

Davey, Lynn. "The Case For A National Testing System." Retrieved November 5, 2012 from (http://PAREonline.net/getvn.asp?v=3&721).

Denton, David. "Finding Alternatives to Failure: Can States End Social Promotion and Retention Rates?" ERIC ED 451268.

"Eleven Facts About Dropping Out." (www. dosomething.org/tipsand tools/11-facts-about-dropping-out#).

Ferrer, Millie and Fugate, Anne. "Helping Your School-Age Child Develop A Healthy Self-Concept." (http://edis.ifas.cfl.edu/fy570)

Fujita, Akiko. "Kids and Laughing Teachers Bullied Suicide Teen" (http://abcnews.go.com/nlogs/head;lines/2012/07 kids-and-laughing-teachers-bullied-teen/).

Gelkham, Yuliya. "The truth about teaching to Standardized tests, Editorial Projects in Education" Education Week, July 21, 2006, (http:// voices.yahoov.com/the-truth-teachng-standardized-tests-54388.html?).

Hauser, Robert M. "Should We End Social Promotion? Truth And Consequences" (www.s5cwis.edu/cdewp/99-06c. pdf). October, 1999. p. 27.

"Helping Your School-Age Child Develop A Healthy Self-Concept." (http:// edis.ifas.ufl.edu/fy570).

"How do schools use standardized tests" (www.fairtest.org how-do-schools= standardized-tests-pdf).

"How Standardized Testing Damages Education, updated July 2012." (www. fairtest.org/how-standardized-testing-damages-education-pdf). July 21, 2006.

Jones, Richard D. "Teaching for Rigor and Relevance" (www.calhounminks. com/uploads/8/2/8/6/8286506/teaching_for_rigor_and_relevance.pdf), February 18, 2011.

Krache, Donna. "Parent Trigger Laws," (http://schoolsofthought.blogs.cnn. com/2012/03/14/five-minute-primer-parent-trigger-laws/).

Kulik, James A. "An Analysis of the Researcg on Ability Grouping: Historical and Contemporary Perspectives." ED350777.

May, Kristen. "What is the Difference Between Self-Concept and Self-Esteem? (http://voices.yahoo.com/what-difference-between-self-concept-self-392531.html?cat=5).

"McCaskill Honors St Louis Judge, Innovative Concept Academy." (http:// mccaskill,senate,gov/?p=press_release&id=1484).

"The Effects On Retention." Consortium on Chicago School Research. (ERIC ED 483835).

Pell, Michael. "More Cheating Scandals Inevitable as States Can't Ensure Test Integrity." (http://www.ajc.com/news/more-cheating-scandals-inevitable-as-states-cant-e/nSPay/).

"Printable Dolch Sight Word List." (http://bogglesworldesl.com/dolch lists.htm).

"Regents Examinations." (http://en.wikipedia.org/wiki/regents-examin-ations).

Rose, Janet S. "A Fresh Look at the Retention-Promotion Controversy." ERIC EJ292730.

Singer, Dale. "Jimmy Edwards uses innovative concepts to give troubled kids one last chance" (www.stbeacon.org/#/content/14441/jimmie-edwards-uses-innovative-concepts-to=give=troubled-kids-one-last-chance).

"Social Promotion". Definition. (http://wn.wikipedia.org/wiki/social pro-motion).

"Students At and Above Grade Level for Reading in Grade 3 Graduate from High School at Higher Rates Than Students Below Grade Level". (www. chapinhall.org/research/inside-students-and-above-grade-level-reading-grade-3-graduates-high-school-higher-rates-stu).

Tanner, John. "The problem with 'rigor' in education" (http://edthink-incap.blogs.com/2008/02-the-problem-with-rigor-in-education.Html).

Thompson, Charles and Cunningham, Elizabeth. "Retention and Social Promotion: Research and Implications for Policy." (www.ericae.net/eda/ed442941.htlm).

"25 Worst Performing Public Schools in the US." (www.dailyfinance.com/photos/worse-performing-public-schools/). page=2), 2009.

Wallace, Robert J. "Science in Elementary Schools" New York University, Math, Science and Technology (MSTEP). (www.divine-caroline.com/34/33707/science-elementary-school).

Weber, Tom. "Why did Minnesota skip the math common core," Minnesota Public Radio , Minnesota Commissioner of Education, Brenda Cassellius. June 12, 2012.

"What is a diploma." The New York Regents Program.

"Why More Standardized Tests Won't Improve Education" (http://parentsacrossamerica.org/why-standardized-tests-won't-improve-education).

www.ingramcontent.com/pod-product-compliance
Lightning Source LLC
Chambersburg PA
CBHW030527100426
42813CB00001B/179